Festival of Holiday PLASTIC CANVAS

Edited by Laura Scott

HOUSE of
WHITE
BIRCHES

PUBLISHERS
SINCE 1947

Festival of Holiday Plastic Canvas

Editor: Laura Scott

Associate Editor: June Sprunger

Copy Editor: Cathy Reef

Assistant to Editorial Director: Jeanne Stauffer

Editorial Director: Vivian Rothe

Photography: Nora Elsesser, Sandy Bauman

Photography Assistant: Linda Quinlan

Production Manager: Vicki Macy

Creative Coordinator: Shaun Venish

Design Director: Scott Ashley

Production Coordinator: Sandra Ridgway Beres

Production Assistants: Patricia Elwell, Cheryl Lynch, Lena Macy, Matthew Martin, Jessica Rothe, Brenda Schneider

Publishers: Carl H. Muselman, Arthur K. Muselman

Chief Executive Officer: John Robinson

Marketing Director: Scott Moss

Printed in the United States of America

First Printing: 1995

Library of Congress Number: 95-78316

ISBN: 1-882138-10-4

Every effort has been made to ensure the accuracy and completeness of the instructions in this book. However, we cannot be responsible for human error or for the results when using materials other than those specified in the instructions, or for variations in individual work.

Cover projects: *Christmas Critters,* pattern begins on Page 118.

Dear Friend,

Every crafter loves to create handmade holiday gifts and decorations. Not only do such handcrafts show an extra amount of effort, but they are also a way for you to give a bit of yourself. Most likely, when you are planning to make gifts for friends, you carefully consider their tastes and personality, and then create gifts to suit them. You'll find a delightful variety of gift ideas for family and friends for every holiday throughout the year.

Just as tastes vary in gift-giving, so home decorating has a different look for each and every home. Whether you prefer a whimsical, fun-loving decor, an elegant look, or anything in between, you are sure to find decorating ideas in the pages that follow to keep your home sparkling all year round.

As editor of this book, it has been a delight to work with the free-lance designers whose original designs grace the pages of this book, and the staff of graphic artists and photographers who have given the projects such a marvelous presentation. It is my hope that this book will not only give you hours of stitching pleasure and creative fulfillment, but that you will also find yourself oftentimes simply browsing through the pages of this book as you would a cherished album.

You'll notice that we have divided up the book into seven chapters. Each chapter includes projects for specific holidays. When you are looking for a quick gift to stitch a sweetheart for Valentine's Day, simply turn to Chapter 1. For Christmas decorating and gift-giving, Chapter 7 will be a priceless source of inspiration! We've also included projects for New Year's Day, St. Patrick's Day, Easter, Mother's Day and Father's Day, Independence Day, Halloween, Thanksgiving and Hanukkah.

I wish each and every one of you many hours of stitching pleasure in creating projects you'll enjoy for years to come.

With warm regards,

Laura Scott

Editor, *Festival of Holiday Plastic Canvas*

Table of Contents

Sweethearts & SHAMROCKS

Winter holidays bring many occasions for festive decorating and gift-giving to chase away the winter chill. Bring in the New Year with family and friends, and be sure to remember your sweetheart on Valentine's Day. And whether you're Irish or not, spry leprechauns and bright sunny rainbows are always a St. Patrick's Day delight!

CONFETTI COASTERS

Designed by Ruth Schmuff

Count down the minutes to the new year with these festive coasters decorated with sparkling numbers and brightly colored confetti.

Skill Level: Beginner

Materials

- 1 sheet 10-count plastic canvas
- #3 pearl cotton as listed in color key
- ⅛" metallic ribbon as listed in color key
- 3½" squares dark violet synthetic suede
- Hot-glue gun

Instructions

1. Cut plastic canvas according to graphs.

2. Stitch pieces following graphs. Overcast edges with black.

3. Glue synthetic suede to back of coasters. ❖

Coasters

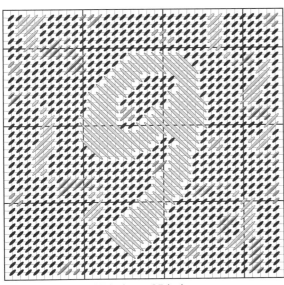

35 holes x 35 holes
Cut 2

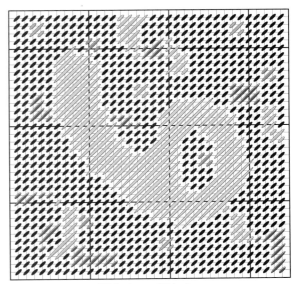

35 holes x 35 holes
Cut 1

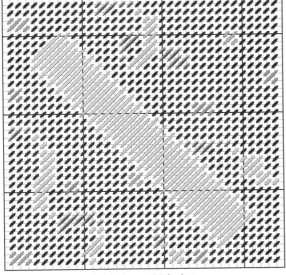

35 holes x 35 holes
Cut 1

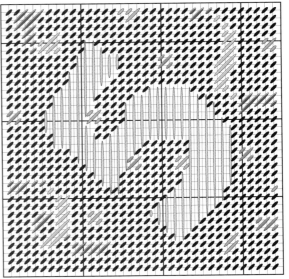

35 holes x 35 holes
Cut 1

October

FALLING SPRINGS MILL
Oregon County, Missouri

1995

SUNDAY	MONDAY	TUESDAY	WEDNESDAY	THURSDAY	FRIDAY	SATURDAY
1 ☽ Second	2	3	4	5	6	7
Sunrise 7:02 Sunset 6:37			Yom Kippur			
8 ○ Full	9	10	11	12	13	14
Harvest Moon	Leave for Vacation					
Sunrise 7:07 Sunset 6:47	Columbus Day					
15	16 ☾ Fourth	17	18	19	20	21
		Home				
Sunrise 7:10 Sunset 6:37						
22	23 ● New	24	25	26	27	28
Sunrise 7:28 Sunset 6:28			Recital			
29	30 ☽ Second	31			September	November
Standard Time–2am				S M T W T F S	S M T W T F S
Sunrise 6:35 Sunset 5:20		Halloween				

A myriad trees sway in the wind, yellow leaves flutter down.
The cold color of mountains all around, I don't open my gate.
Someone once planted these cedars in the garden
Just to keep half a day's sunshine from these thatched eaves.

DAY-BY-DAY CALENDAR

Designed by Mary T. Cosgrove

Skill Level: Beginner

Materials
- 2 sheets stiff 7-count plastic canvas*
- Plastic canvas yarn* as listed in color key

Instructions

1. Cut plastic canvas according to graphs (Page 12). Calendar holder back will remain unstitched.

2. Stitch pieces following graphs. Overcast numbers with beige. With burgundy, Whip-stitch calendar holder front and back pieces together along both inside and outside edges.

3. Cut four 4" lengths of beige yarn. Using one length of yarn per number, Continental Stitch numbers to calendar holder where indicated on graphs. Tie a small knot at back; trim ends.

4. To hang, cut a 12" length of beige yarn. Slide ends of yarn through burgundy stitches at back of calendar where indicated on graph; knot ends. ❖

This country calendar holder is perfect for year-after-year use. Simply slide a calendar into the opening and stitch the appropriate year!

Day-by-Day Calendar

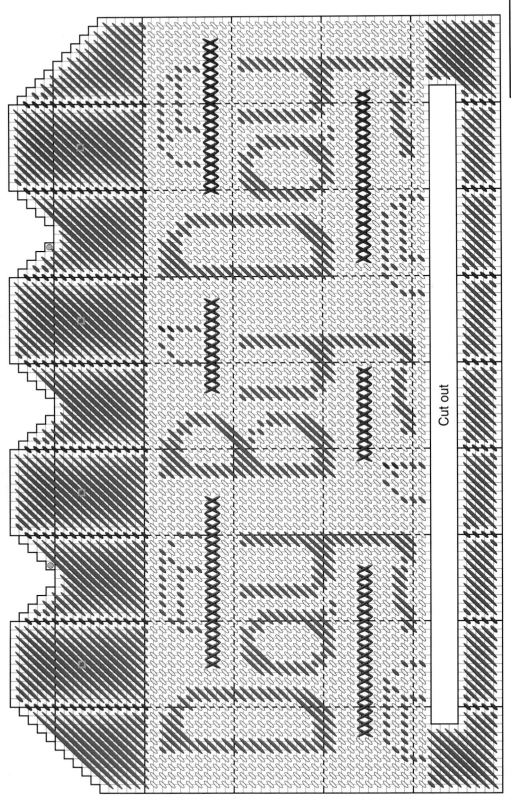

Calendar Holder Front & Back
90 holes x 55 holes
Cut 2, leaving back unstitched

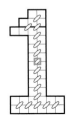

6 holes x 12 holes
Cut 1

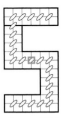

6 holes x 12 holes
Cut 1

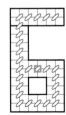

6 holes x 12 holes
Cut 1

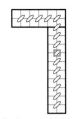

6 holes x 12 holes
Cut 1

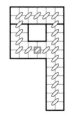

6 holes x 12 holes
Cut 2

Love Notes

Leave a romantic message for your sweetie with one of these quick-to-stitch love note magnets.

Designed by Nancy Marshall

Skill Level: Beginner

Materials

- ¼ sheet 7-count plastic canvas
- Plastic canvas yarn as listed in color key
- 3 (1") magnetic strips
- Hot-glue gun

Instructions

1. Cut plastic canvas according to graphs.

2. Stitch notes following graphs. Overcast with red.

3. Glue one magnet to back of each heart. ❖

COLOR KEY	
Plastic Canvas Yarn	**Yards**
■ Christmas red #19	6
Color number given is for Darice Nylon Plus plastic canvas yarn.	

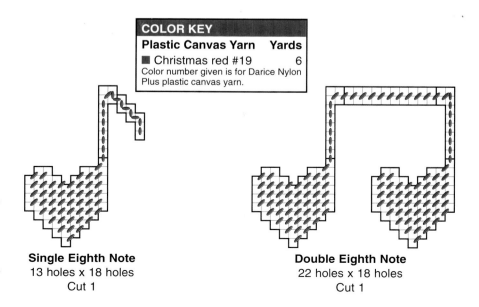

Single Eighth Note
13 holes x 18 holes
Cut 1

Double Eighth Note
22 holes x 18 holes
Cut 1

VALENTINE CUPIDS

Designed by Michele Wilcox

The cupids on the sides of this tissue box cover are searching for their next pair of sweethearts! Will it be you and someone special?

Skill Level: Beginner

Materials

- 1¼ sheets 7-count plastic canvas
- Plastic canvas yarn as listed in color key

Instructions

1. Cut plastic canvas according to graphs.

2. Stitch pieces following graphs.

3. Overcast bottom side edges and inner edge of top with white. With white, Whipstitch sides together and then top to sides. ❖

COLOR KEY	
Plastic Canvas Yarn	**Yards**
☐ White #41	65
■ Crimson #42	50
Color numbers given are for Uniek Needloft plastic canvas yarn.	

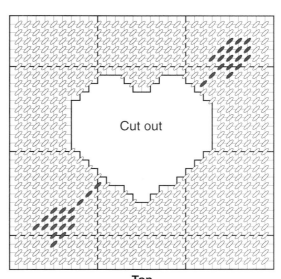

Top
30 holes x 30 holes
Cut 1

Side
30 holes x 36 holes
Cut 1

Give this beautiful heart-shaped keepsake box to your sweetheart with a special Valentine's Day gift tucked inside.

Forever Yours KEEPSAKE BOX

Designed by Kathy Wirth

Skill Level: Intermediate

Materials

- 2 (6") plastic canvas hearts
- ¼ sheet clear 7-count plastic canvas
- ¼ sheet ivory 7-count plastic canvas
- Plastic canvas yarn as listed in color key
- ⅛"-wide metallic ribbon as listed in color key
- 1 yard ¼"-wide red double-face satin ribbon
- 1 sheet self-adhesive red felt
- 1⅛"-wide gold heart charm
- #18 tapestry needle
- Clear nylon monofilament

Instructions

1. Cut plastic canvas according to graph. Cut outer bar off one plastic canvas heart for box bottom. Cut two 62-hole x 8-hole pieces from ivory plastic canvas for box sides. Cut out bars on lid top as indicated on graph.

2. Stitch pieces following graphs. For lid top, weave ribbon in and out of slits, leaving long tails at center top.

3. Using box bottom as a template, cut heart shape from felt so felt fits just inside outer bar of heart. Set aside.

4. With right sides together, Whipstitch one short edge of lid sides together with wine. With wrong sides together, Whipstitch remaining short edges together with wine so heart shape is formed. Repeat for box sides, Whipstitching short edges together with monofilament.

5. Whipstitch lid top to lid sides

with gold; Overcast bottom edges of lid sides with gold. Whipstitch box sides to box bottom with gold; Overcast top edges of box sides with gold.

6. Peel backing from felt heart and place in bottom of box.

7. Thread charm onto one satin ribbon tail. Tie ribbon in bow; trim ends evenly. ❖

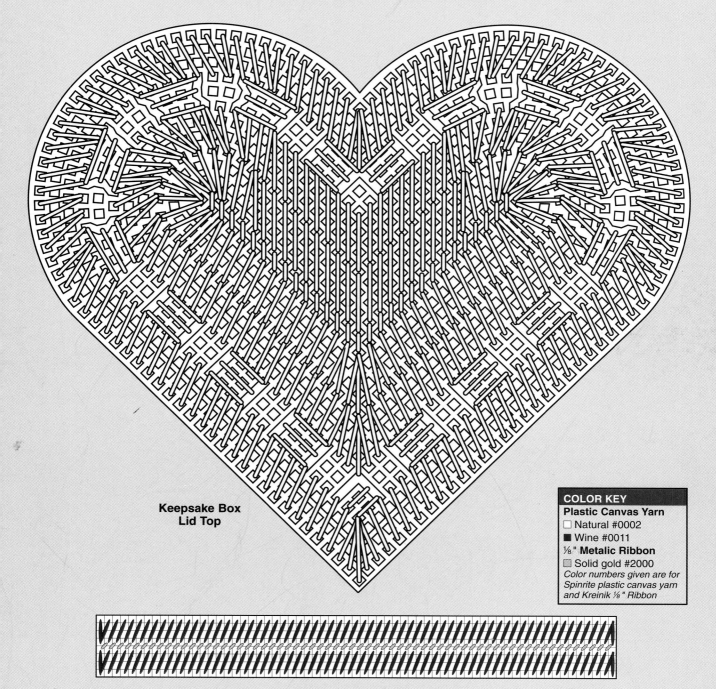

Keepsake Box Lid Top

Keepsake Box Lid Side
65 holes x 8 holes
Cut 2

Fill this pretty valentine basket with colorful conversation hearts. Take it to work for a treat for your co-workers, or keep it at home for your hubby and kids!

CANDY HEARTS FOR SWEETHEARTS

Designed by Michele Wilcox

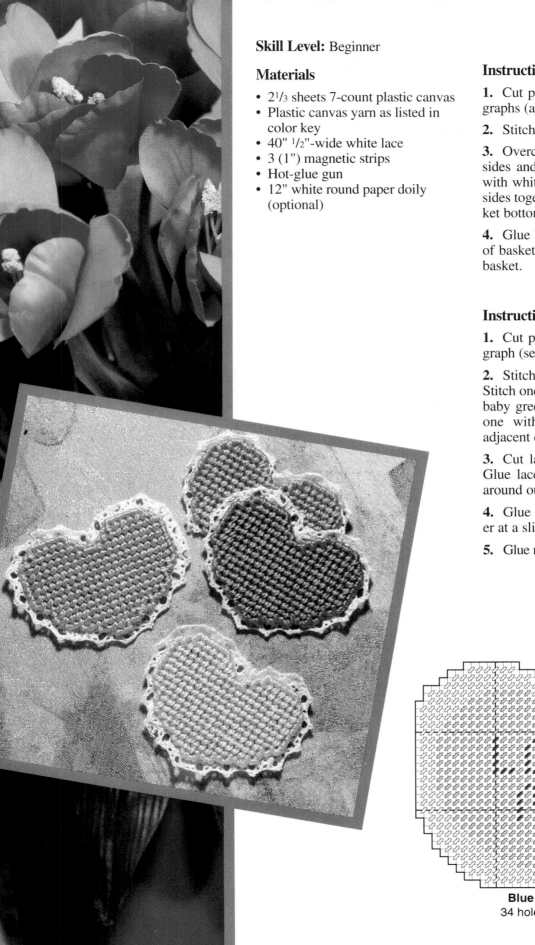

Skill Level: Beginner

Materials

- 2¹/₃ sheets 7-count plastic canvas
- Plastic canvas yarn as listed in color key
- 40" ¹/₂"-wide white lace
- 3 (1") magnetic strips
- Hot-glue gun
- 12" white round paper doily (optional)

Basket

Instructions

1. Cut plastic canvas according to graphs (also see Page 20).

2. Stitch pieces following graphs.

3. Overcast top edges of basket sides and all four edges of handle with white. With white, Whipstitch sides together and then sides to basket bottom.

4. Glue handle to top inside edges of basket. If desired, place doily in basket.

Magnets

Instructions

1. Cut plastic canvas according to graph (see Page 20).

2. Stitch hearts following graphs. Stitch one heart with pink, one with baby green, one with sail blue and one with yellow. Overcast with adjacent colors.

3. Cut lace into four 10" lengths. Glue lace to wrong side of hearts around outer edge.

4. Glue one heart on top of another at a slight angle.

5. Glue magnets to back of hearts. ❖

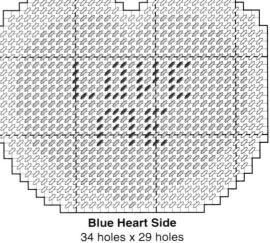

Blue Heart Side
34 holes x 29 holes
Cut 1

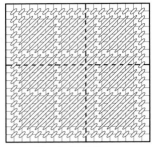

Basket Bottom
18 holes x 18 holes
Cut 1

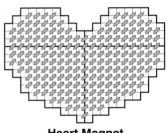

Heart Magnet
20 holes x 15 holes
Cut 4
Stitch 1 with pink, 1 with baby green
1 with sail blue, 1 with yellow

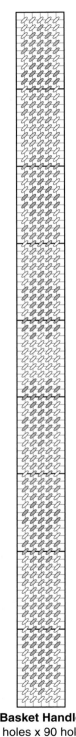

Basket Handle
6 holes x 90 holes
Cut 1

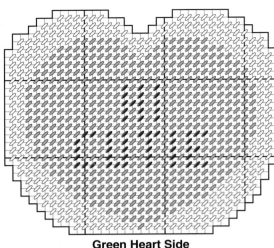

Green Heart Side
34 holes x 29 holes
Cut 1

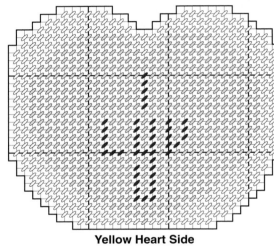

Yellow Heart Side
34 holes x 29 holes
Cut 1

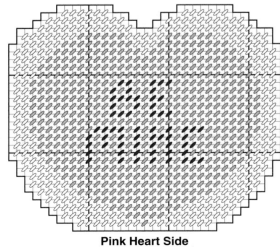

Pink Heart Side
34 holes x 29 holes
Cut 1

Whip up a set of festive shamrock napkin rings in just minutes for a St. Paddy's party!

SPARKLING SHAMROCKS

Designed by Joan Green

Skill Level: Beginner

Materials

For 1 napkin ring

- 1/12 sheet 7-count plastic canvas
- Plastic canvas yarn as listed in color key
- 1 1/2 yards metallic green plastic canvas yarn #7
- #16 tapestry needle

Instructions

1. Cut plastic canvas according to graph.

2. Stitch shamrock following graph. Overcast inner edges with clover and outer edges with metallic green yarn. ❖

COLOR KEY	
Plastic Canvas Yarn	**Yards**
▨ Clover #42	3
Color number given is for Spinrite plastic canvas yarn.	

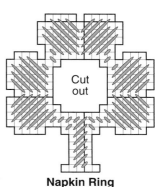

Napkin Ring
19 holes x 21 holes
Cut 1

Leprechaun

These three leprechauns have struck it rich! Surrounded by blooming shamrocks and sparkling pieces of gold each collects a treasure in his hat.

Skill Level: Advanced

Materials

- 2 artist-size sheets 7-count plastic canvas
- 6" plastic canvas circle
- Plastic canvas yarn as listed in color key
- Metallic cord as listed in color key
- 8" x 12" piece dark green felt
- 6 small gold beads
- 16 white silk flowers
- Green sewing thread and needle
- Hot-glue gun
- 3 1/2"-diameter x 3 5/8"-tall empty frosting container (optional)

Project Note

Read all instructions before beginning.

Cutting & Stitching

1. Cut plastic canvas according to graphs (Pages 24 and 25). For pot brim, cut out center of 6" circle so only the outer seven bars remain. Stitch all pieces following graphs and steps below.

2. For leprechauns, reverse one arm and one leg for each leprechaun before stitching; Overcast with adjacent colors. Overcast nose with flesh tone.

3. For the head, leave shaded gray area on head back unstitched. Stitch mouths following Fig. 1. Stitch French Knot eyes with royal blue. With flesh tone, stitch lower face front together at darts and then lower head back together at darts to shape head. Overcast ears on face front with flesh tone. On head back, Overcast top of head between dots and behind ears between dots with flesh tone.

4. With bittersweet, stitch 1 1/2"-long Turkey Loops for hair and beard on face. Cut loops, trim and fluff. With flesh tone, stitch nose to face where indicated on graph. With flesh tone, Whipstitch face and head back together along all unstitched edges and at bottom of face directly below beard.

5. When stitching body pieces, stitch darts together at top and bottom with avocado. With avocado, Whipstitch body fronts to body backs, leaving neck area open for insertion of head.

Continued on page 26

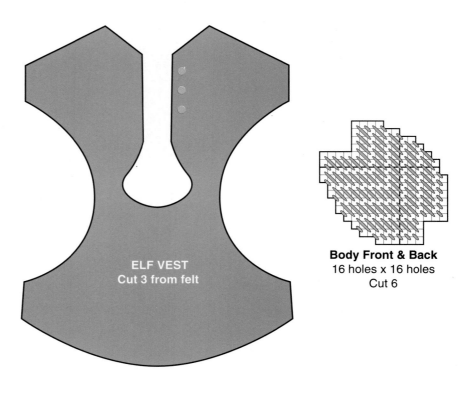

ELF VEST
Cut 3 from felt

Body Front & Back
16 holes x 16 holes
Cut 6

Fig. 1

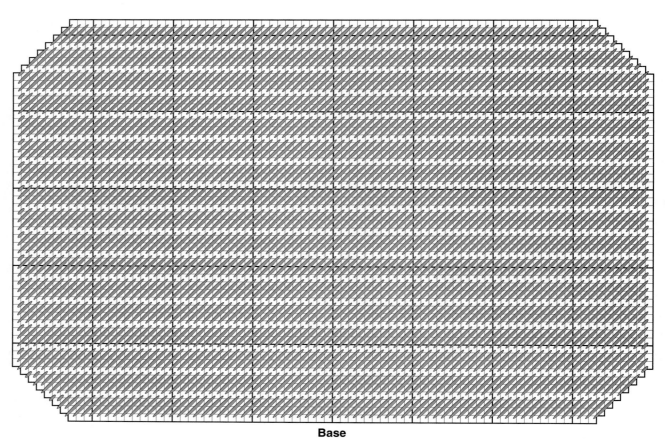

Base
80 holes x 52 holes
Cut 2, stitch 1

24

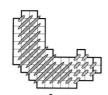

Arm
11 holes x 10 holes
Cut 6, reverse 3 before sitching

Leg
9 holes x 15 holes
Cut 6, reverse 3 before sitching

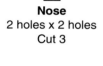

Face
14 holes x 14 holes
Cut 3

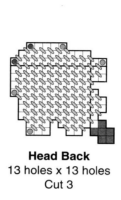

Head Back
13 holes x 13 holes
Cut 3

Nose
2 holes x 2 holes
Cut 3

Gold Coin
4 holes x 4 holes
Cut 10

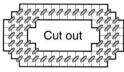

Cut out

Hat Brim
15 holes x 8 holes
Cut 3

Hat Top
10 holes x 4 holes
Cut 3

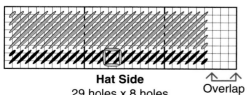

Hat Side
29 holes x 8 holes
Cut 3

Overlap

Shamrock
8 holes x 7 holes
Cut 7

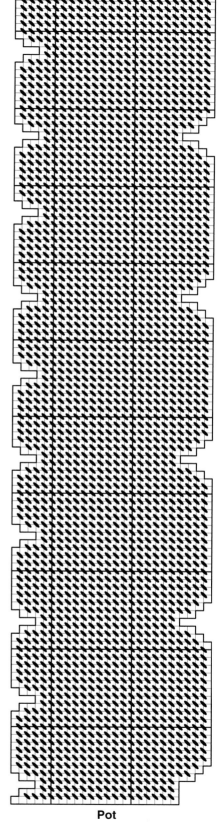

Pot
108 holes x 25 holes
Cut 1

Leprechaun Party

Continued from Page 23

6. For hats, stitch gold buckles on hat sides over black stitches. Overcast brim edge of hat sides and both inner and outer brim edges with avocado. As indicated on graph, overlap holes on hat sides then Whipstitch together with avocado. With avocado, Whipstitch hat top to hat side.

7. For base, add loops of grass to stitched piece (see photo). Whipstitch unstitched base to stitched piece with holly green.

8. For pot, stitch darts together with black. With black, Straight Stitch pot brim from inner holes to last row of holes along outside edge, using two stitches per hole when necessary. Overcast edges of pot brim with black.

9. Overcast shamrocks and gold coins with adjacent colors.

Finishing

1. Insert neck of head into body.

2. Using vest pattern (Page 24), cut three vests from dark green felt. Sew narrow side seams of each vest together. Sew gold beads on vest fronts for buttons. Place vests on elves.

3. With avocado, tack arms to upper body sides. Using photo as a guide, with avocado, sew legs to lower body sides so one leprechaun can sit on grass, one can stand and one can sit on pot brim with left leg hanging over edge.

4. Glue hat brims to hats. Glue pot rim to top of pot.

5. Using photo as a guide, glue pot to base. Glue one leprechaun to pot brim, then one flower and one shamrock to one hand and gold coin to other. Glue one hat right side up to brim of pot and one gold coin to edge of hat brim.

6. Glue sitting elf to right front of base then glue hat, with brim on top, between his legs. Arrange bouquet of flowers in hat and glue to secure. Reserve several flowers for later.

7. Glue standing elf behind sitting elf. Glue hat with brim on top to one elf's hand and arm. Glue one gold coin in other hand. Arrange three coins in hat; glue in place. Glue one coin to edge of hat brim.

8. Using photo as a guide, glue shamrocks, gold coins and flowers as desired on base.

9. Fill pot with candy or insert empty frosting container into pot and then fill. ❖

LUCKY

Designed by Mary T. Cosgrove

Skill Level: Beginner

Materials

- ¼ sheet 7-count plastic canvas
- Plastic canvas yarn as listed in color key
- Plastic canvas cord as listed in color key
- Heavy (#32) metallic braid as listed in color key
- Plastic jar with green heart-shaped lid
- 2 (7mm) wiggly eyes
- Jewel glue
- Hot-glue gun

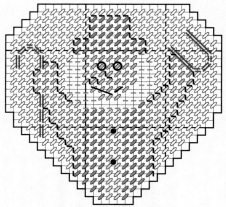

Lucky the Leprechaun Lid
27 holes x 26 holes
Cut 1

COLOR KEY	
Plastic Canvas Yarn	**Yards**
▨ Pink #07	1
☐ White #41	5
☐ Yellow #57	2
╱ Maple #13 Backstitch	1
╱ Yellow #57 Backstitch	
− Bright orange #58 Turkey Loop	2
Plastic Canvas Cord	
▨ Green #04	
Heavy (#32) Metallic Braid	
╱ Black #005HL Backstitch and Straight Stitch	2
● Black #005HL French Knot	
○ Attach eyes	
Color numbers given are for Uniek Needloft plastic canvas yarn and plastic canvas cord and Kreinik Heavy (#32) Braid.	

THE LEPRECHAUN

This clever goodie jar will delight your Irish friends all year round! Fill it with a favorite treat as a festive St. Patrick's Day gift.

Instructions

1. Cut plastic canvas according to graph.

2. Continental Stitch following graph. With yellow, Backstitch buckle on hat. Outline leprechaun with black Backstitches. Stitch nose, mouth and pipe with black Straight Stitches. Add black French Knots for buttons.

3. Using two Straight Stitches per hole, stitch horseshoe and cane with maple over white Continental Stitches.

4. For beard, stitch orange Turkey Loops. Cut loops, fray ends and trim.

5. Overcast edges with white. Using jewel glue, attach wiggly eyes where indicated on graph.

6. Glue back of finished canvas piece to plastic insert. Place in heart-shaped lid. ❖

PROUD TO BE

This coffee mug will encourage Irish pride!

A colorful rainbow and kelly green shamrocks will take you to the Emerald Isle.

Designed by Darla J. Fanton

Skill Level: Beginner

Materials

- ½ sheet 10-count plastic canvas
- #3 pearl cotton as listed in color key
- Green stitchery mug

Instructions

1. Cut plastic canvas according to graph.

2. Stitch piece following graph, working Continental Stitches first, then Backstitches on top of Continental Stitches. Uncoded areas are white Continental Stitches.

3. Overcast long edges with white. Whipstitch short edges together with white.

4. Insert stitched piece in mug with joined edge at handle. ❖

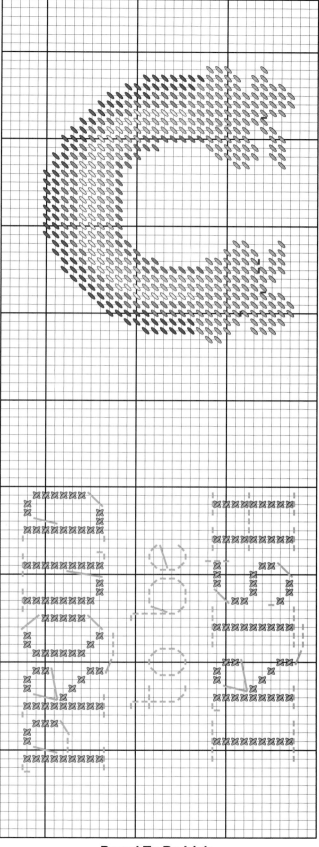

COLOR KEY	
#3 Pearl Cotton	**Yards**
■ Christmas red #321	31
☐ Deep canary #444	1
■ Dark lavender #554	1
☐ Light blue #813	1
■ Christmas green #909	1
■ Bright pumpkin #947	7
╱ Light blue #813 Backstitch	1
╱ Christmas green #909 Backstitch	
╱ White Backstitch	

Uncoded areas are white Continental Stitches
Color numbers given are for DMC #3 pearl cotton.

Proud To Be Irish
96 holes x 35 holes
Cut 1

"At the end of every rainbow is a leprechaun's pot of gold," says a favorite Irish story. Fill this pot with gold-foil–covered chocolates for a St. Patrick's Day delight!

POT O' GOLD CANDY DISH

Designed by Celia Lange Designs

Skill Level: Beginner

Materials

- 2 sheets 7-count plastic canvas
- ½ sheet 10-count plastic canvas
- Plastic canvas yarn as listed in color key
- Metallic braid ribbon as listed in color key
- 1 yard ¼"-wide antique gold metallic braid ribbon
- 1 yard ¼"-wide emerald satin ribbon
- Metallic braid as listed in color key
- Metallic thread as listed in color key
- Low-temp glue gun

Instructions

1. Cut plastic canvas according to graphs.

2. Stitch pieces following graphs. Overcast harp and shamrock with adjacent colors. When stitching is completed on harp, thread harp string following graph.

3. Overcast handle edges with black. With black, Whipstitch side and corner pieces together and then sides to bottom. Overcast top edges of pot with black.

4. Where indicated with red dots on graph, stitch handles to sides with black using one or two stitches to se-

cure, making sure handles curve up.

5. Hold emerald ribbon and ¼"-wide gold braid ribbon together, twist, then tie around pot so shamrock will cover ends (see photo). Glue shamrock over ribbon ends and then glue harp to front center of shamrock. ❖

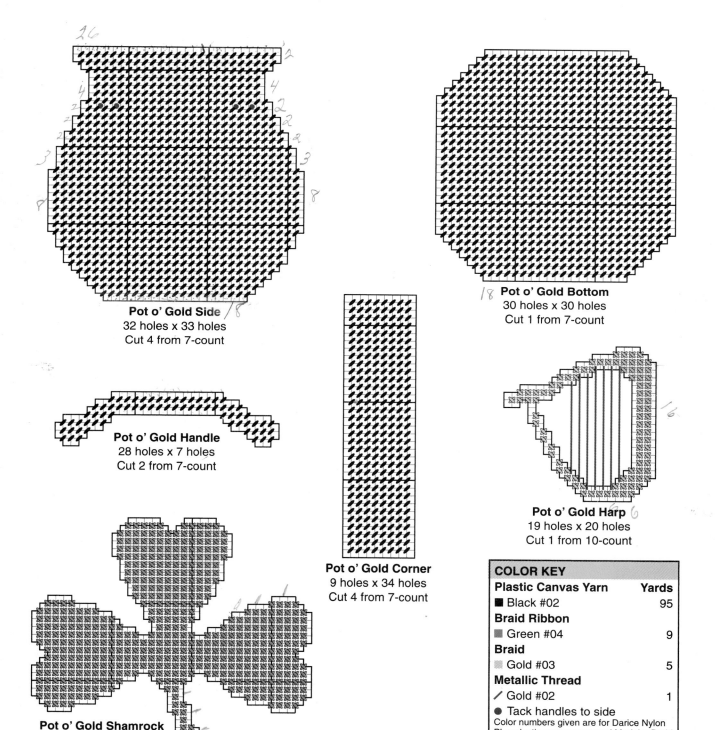

Pot o' Gold Side
32 holes x 33 holes
Cut 4 from 7-count

Pot o' Gold Bottom
30 holes x 30 holes
Cut 1 from 7-count

Pot o' Gold Handle
28 holes x 7 holes
Cut 2 from 7-count

Pot o' Gold Corner
9 holes x 34 holes
Cut 4 from 7-count

Pot o' Gold Harp
19 holes x 20 holes
Cut 1 from 10-count

Pot o' Gold Shamrock
35 holes x 31 holes
Cut 1 from 10-count

COLOR KEY	
Plastic Canvas Yarn	**Yards**
■ Black #02	95
Braid Ribbon	
■ Green #04	9
Braid	
▧ Gold #03	5
Metallic Thread	
╱ Gold #02	1
● Tack handles to side	

Color numbers given are for Darice Nylon Plus plastic canvas yarn and Madeira Braid Ribbon 2, Braid and Glimmer metallic thread.

EASTER DELIGHTS

Along with the welcomed blooms of crocuses, daffodils, irises, tulips and lilacs comes the colorful and cheerful spring holiday of Easter. In this chapter, you'll discover dozens of decorating and gift-giving ideas for Easter, all in sunny colors and adorable settings.

Delight children with three lovable critters peeking out from inside pastel-colored, sparkly Easter eggs!

Easter Egg Surprise

Designed by Vicki Blizzard

Skill Level: Beginner

Materials

- 1 sheet 7-count plastic canvas
- Plastic canvas yarn as listed in color key
- 6 (6mm) black round cabochons
- 4mm black round cabochon
- Approximately 45 (3mm) aurora borealis crystal rhinestones
- Heat-set tool (for setting rhinestones)
- 6" each ⅛"-wide satin ribbon: peach, baby blue and baby yellow
- #16 tapestry needle
- 6 (1") lengths magnet strips
- Hot-glue gun

Instructions

1. Cut plastic canvas according to graphs.

2. Stitch pieces following graphs. Continental Stitch one egg with sky for chick, one egg with pale pink for duck and one egg with seafoam for bunny. Overcast pieces with adjacent colors. Continental Stitch one head with lemon for chick, one with white for duck and one with silver gray for bunny. Overcast with adjacent colors.

3. Use 2 strands yarn to stitch and Overcast flowers. Using 4 strands lemon, add French Knots to center of blue flowers. Overcast remaining pieces with adjacent colors, except for bunny's ears which are Overcast with silver gray. Whipstitch inside of bunny's ears together with pale pink.

4. For Straight Stitching on bunny's muzzle, use 2 strands cherry blossom. Glue peach flowers to sky egg as desired, using photo as a guide. Straight Stitch stems of flowers as desired using 2 strands seafoam.

5. Attach short lengths of white yarn to center top of duck head and short lengths of lemon yarn to center top of chick head, fray ends and trim.

6. Using photo as a guide, glue 6mm cabochons to heads for eyes. Glue 4mm cabochon to bunny's muzzle for nose. Glue bunny muzzle, duck bill and chick beak to heads. If desired, place a dot of glue on inside back of chick beak and duck bill; hold together until set.

7. Using photo as a guide, glue heads to backs of egg bottoms then egg tops to heads and egg bottoms. Glue flowers and leaves to eggs as desired, using photo as a guide.

8. Tie ribbons into small bows; trim ends. Glue peach bow to top of chick's head, baby blue ribbon to side of duck's head and baby yellow bow to bottom side of bunny's head.

9. Using heat-set tool, apply rhinestones to eggs as desired to resemble drops of dew. Glue magnet strips to backs of egg tops and bottoms. ❖

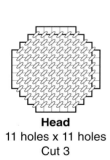

Head
11 holes x 11 holes
Cut 3

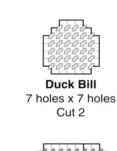

Duck Bill
7 holes x 7 holes
Cut 2

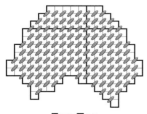

Egg Top
17 holes x 13 holes
Cut 3

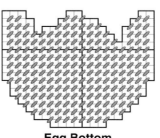

Egg Bottom
19 holes x 15 holes
Cut 3

Bunny Muzzle
7 holes x 4 holes
Cut 1

Chick Beak
5 holes x 4 holes
Cut 2

Duck Leaf
5 holes x 6 holes
Cut 4

Chick Flower
2 holes x 2 holes
Cut 12

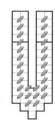

Bunny Ear
5 holes x 14 holes
Cut 2

Bunny Flower Top
3 holes x 3 holes
Cut 6

Bunny Flower Base
5 holes x 5 holes
Cut 6

Duck Flower
3 holes x 3 holes
Cut 5

COLOR KEY	
Plastic Canvas Yarn	**Yards**
☐ White #0001	3
▦ Pale pink #0003	10
☐ Sky #0004	9
☐ Lemon #0006	4
▨ Peach #0007	2
▩ Cherry blossom #0010	1
▦ Seafoam #0013	9
☐ Daffodil #0029	3
▨ Silver gray #0045	3
╱ Cherry blossom #0010 Straight Stitch	
Color numbers given are for Spinrite plastic canvas yarn.	

EASTER EGG HUNT

Designed by Dianne Davis

Look who's found a colored egg in the flower garden! This delightful bunny amidst pretty spring blooms makes a perfect basket for your Easter egg hunt!

Skill Level: Beginner

Materials

- 2½ sheets 7-count plastic canvas
- Plastic canvas yarn as listed in color key
- 6-strand embroidery floss as listed in color key
- #16 or #18 tapestry needle

Instructions

1. Cut plastic canvas according to graphs. Cut one 36-hole x 36-hole piece for basket bottom, which will remain unstitched.

2. Following graphs, stitch front and back pieces with Continental, Cross, Gobelin and Condensed Mosaic Stitches. Backstitch flower stems with mermaid green. Use 3 strands floss for gray Backstitching. For bunny's tail, make Turkey Loops ½" long; clip loops and trim to round tail.

3. Following graphs, stitch sides with Brighton and Cross Stitches and handle with Condensed Mosaic Stitches.

4. Overcast top edges of front and back and long edges of basket han-dle with baby green. With baby green, Overcast top edges of sides, leaving area where handle will be attached unstitched. With baby green, Whipstitch basket sides together and then sides to un-stitched bottom. Whipstitch handle to sides where indicated on graph.

5. Cut two 12" lengths of pink yarn. On one side, insert one length of yarn at blue dot. Bring yarn out at second blue dot. Tie yarn in small bow, trimming ends as desired. Repeat for other side. ❖

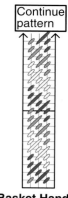

Basket Handle
4 holes x 90 holes
Cut 1

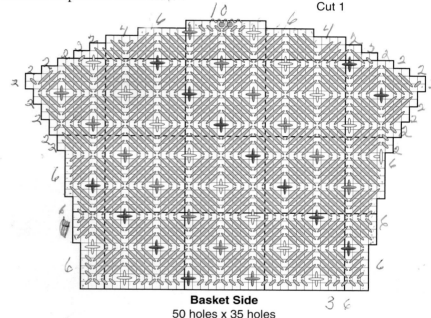

Basket Side
50 holes x 35 holes
Cut 2

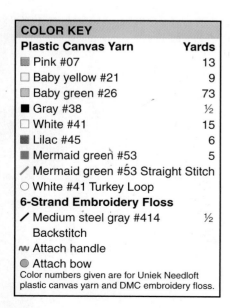

COLOR KEY	
Plastic Canvas Yarn	**Yards**
Pink #07	13
Baby yellow #21	9
Baby green #26	73
Gray #38	½
White #41	15
Lilac #45	6
Mermaid green #53	5
Mermaid green #53 Straight Stitch	
White #41 Turkey Loop	
6-Strand Embroidery Floss	
Medium steel gray #414 Backstitch	½
Attach handle	
Attach bow	

Color numbers given are for Uniek Needloft plastic canvas yarn and DMC embroidery floss.

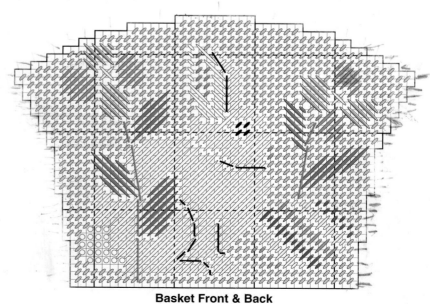

Basket Front & Back
50 holes x 35 holes
Cut 2

BUNNY & CHICK BASKET BUDDIES

Designed by Nancy Marshall

Delight your kids or grandkids with special treats served up in one of these whimsical baby animal gift baskets!

Skill Level: Beginner

Materials

- 2 sheets clear 7-count plastic canvas
- Plastic canvas yarn as listed in color key
- 6-strand embroidery floss as listed in color key
- 1" pink pompon
- Craft glue

Instructions

1. Cut plastic canvas according to graphs. Cut one 21-hole x 15-hole piece for each base.

2. Stitch pieces following graphs. Stitch box backs and sides using silver for bunny basket and yellow for chick basket. Whipstitch beak pieces together along straight edge with burnt orange. Do not stitch base pieces. Use 6 strands floss for Cross Stitches and Backstitches.

3. Overcast top edges of each piece with adjacent colors. Whipstitch sides to fronts and backs with adjacent colors. Whipstitch base pieces to sides with adjacent colors.

4. Glue pink pompon on bunny for nose. Glue joined edge of beak to chick between cheeks. ❖

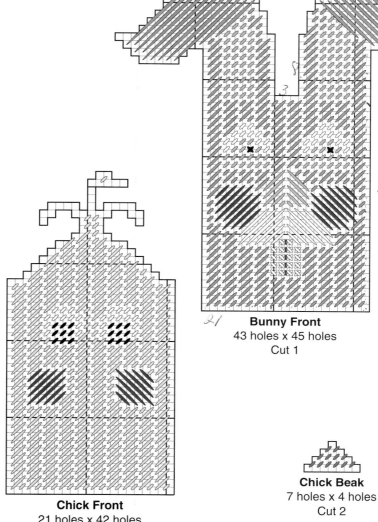

Bunny Front
43 holes x 45 holes
Cut 1

Chick Front
21 holes x 42 holes
Cut 1

Chick Beak
7 holes x 4 holes
Cut 2

COLOR KEY	
BUNNY BOX	
Plastic Canvas Yarn	**Yards**
☐ White #01	1½
■ Black #02	½
▨ Sail blue #04	1
▨ Powder pink #11	2
▨ Silver #40	32
■ Watermelon #54	1
Embroidery Floss	
☐ White	1
╱ Black #310 Backstitch	⅓
CHICK BOX	
Plastic Canvas Yarn	**Yards**
☐ White #01	½
■ Black #02	½
▨ Burnt orange #17	1
☐ Yellow #26	18½
■ Watermelon #54	1

Color numbers given are for Darice Nylon Plus plastic canvas yarn and DMC embroidery floss.

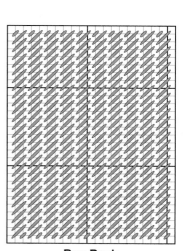

Box Side
15 holes x 28 holes
Cut 2 for each box

Box Back
21 holes x 28 holes
Cut 1 for each box

Eggs in a Basket

Designed by Nancy Marshall

Add a festive touch to your Easter brunch with these colorful Easter egg coasters and coordinating basket holder!

Skill Level: Beginner

Materials

- 1¼ sheets 7-count plastic canvas
- Plastic canvas yarn as listed in color key
- Straw satin raffia as listed in color key
- Tapestry needle
- Easter grass
- Hot-glue gun

Instructions

1. Cut plastic canvas according to graphs. Cut one 35-hole x 11-hole piece for basket bottom.

2. Stitch basket pieces following graphs; basket bottom will remain unstitched. Overcast top edges of sides and long edges of handle with tan. With tan, Whipstitch sides together and then sides to bottom. With tan, Whipstitch handle to basket sides where indicated on graph.

3. Glue Easter grass around inside top edge of basket.

4. For coasters, following graphs, stitch tangerine Gobelin Stitches and Diamond Eyelet Stitches first.

5. For one egg, fill in center section, B, with lilac Continental Stitches and remaining top and bottom sections, A, with purple Continental Stitches. Work Long Stitches in section B with purple.

6. For second egg, Continental Stitch section B with moss and sections A with holly green. Work Long Stitches in section B with holly green.

7. For third egg, Continental Stitch section B with sail blue and sections A with royal blue. Work Long Stitches in section B with royal blue.

8. For last egg, Continental Stitch section B with powder pink and sections A with watermelon. Work Long Stitches in section B with watermelon.

9. Overcast eggs with adjacent colors and place in basket. ❖

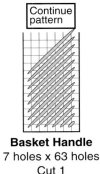

Basket Handle
7 holes x 63 holes
Cut 1

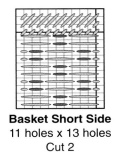

Basket Short Side
11 holes x 13 holes
Cut 2

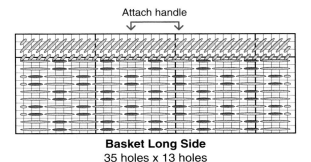

Attach handle

Basket Long Side
35 holes x 13 holes
Cut 2

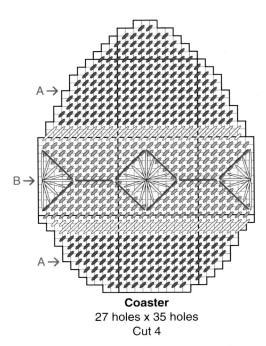

Coaster
27 holes x 35 holes
Cut 4

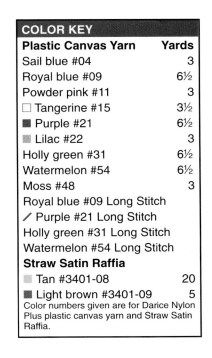

COLOR KEY	
Plastic Canvas Yarn	**Yards**
Sail blue #04	3
Royal blue #09	6½
Powder pink #11	3
☐ Tangerine #15	3½
■ Purple #21	6½
▨ Lilac #22	3
Holly green #31	6½
Watermelon #54	6½
Moss #48	3
Royal blue #09 Long Stitch	
╱ Purple #21 Long Stitch	
Holly green #31 Long Stitch	
Watermelon #54 Long Stitch	
Straw Satin Raffia	
▨ Tan #3401-08	20
■ Light brown #3401-09	5
Color numbers given are for Darice Nylon Plus plastic canvas yarn and Straw Satin Raffia.	

JELLY BEAN BU[NNIES]

Delight jelly bean lovers with one of these adorable bunny candy cups filled with mini jelly beans!

Designed by Adele Mogavero

Skill Level: Intermediate

Materials

- 4 sheets 7-count plastic canvas
- 4-ply worsted weight yarn as listed in color key
- #16 tapestry needle
- 8 (12mm) oval wiggle eyes
- 12 (1"-wide) white pompons
- 4 (½"-wide) pink pompons
- 8 (7mm) dark sapphire round frosted cabochons
- 1⅓ yard ¼"-wide satin ribbon: lilac or coordinating colors
- Low-temp glue gun

Project Note

To make extra jelly bean cups, yarn amounts for one standing bunny are: 20 yards white, 15 yards clothing color, 10 yards basket color and 3 yards pink. Yarn amounts for one sitting bunny are: 20 yards white, 25 yards clothing and matching basket color and 5 yards pink.

Cutting & Stitching

1. Cut pieces following graphs (also see Page 47), noting cutting line for sitting bunnies.

2. Stitch pieces following graphs. Basket bottoms will remain unstitched. Reverse eight arms before stitching.

3. Stitch one basket and handle with lilac, one with light mint, one with petal pink and one with pale yellow.

4. Stitch overalls on front and back pieces of one standing bunny in light blue and overalls on front and back pieces of remaining standing bunny in pale yellow. Stitch overalls on front and back pieces of one sitting bunny in light mint and overalls on front and back pieces of remaining sitting bunny in lilac.

5. For overall straps, using 6½" lengths of two strands matching yarn and with bunny back right side up, bring needle down through one hole at dot indicated on graph and up at second dot. Make yarn ends even, tie in bow to keep out of the way and set aside.

6. With wrong sides of two arm pieces together, Whipstitch all edges together, except for straight edge,
with white. Repeat for remaining seven arms.

7. With wrong sides of body fronts and backs together and using white, Whipstitch arms to body sides where indicated on graphs, stitching through all thicknesses. Whipstitch remaining edges of bodies together with adjacent colors. Overcast feet with white.

8. Whipstitch short ends of basket sides together and then basket bottoms to sides with matching colors. Overcast top edges of baskets and long edges of handles with matching colors. With matching colors, Whipstitch ends of handles to sides of baskets.

Assembly

1. For each bunny, using photo as a guide, glue two 1"-wide pompons side by side to bottom of face for muzzle. Glue one ½"-wide pink pompon to center top of muzzle. Glue oval wiggle eyes above muzzle.

2. For overall straps, untie bows, cross yarn in back and bring to front. Glue straps to top of overalls. Cut excess yarn close to glued area. Glue a cabochon on top of each strap, covering ends of yarn. Glue one 1"-wide pompon to center bottoms of backs for tails.

3. For each standing bunny, glue bottom edge of body to feet where indicated on graph. Center and glue bottom of petal pink basket to top of feet of bunny with yellow overalls, positioning basket so handle can be glued to paws; glue paws to handle. Repeat for bunny with light blue overalls, using pale yellow basket.

4. Cut ribbon into four equal lengths, tie each length in a bow and glue bow to each side of standing bunny's basket at handle edge. Trim tails of bows to desire length.

5. For each sitting bunny, center and glue basket of matching color to body front, keeping bottom of basket even with bottom edge of bunny and positioning basket handles as for standing bunny. Glue hands to basket and handle.

6. Using photo as a guide, glue wrong sides of bunny feet in a diagonal position to fronts of baskets. ❖

ELEGANT EMB[...]

Designed by Celia Lange Designs

Try your hand at a beautiful technique called ribbon embroidery while making a set of nine pretty Easter eggs to hang on an Easter tree!

Skill Level: Intermediate

Materials

- 1 sheet 10-count plastic canvas
- #5 pearl cotton:
  14 yards snow white
  7 yards shaded roses
  7 yards shaded yellows
  7 yards shaded bright greens
  10½ yards light lavender
  3½ yards very light cranberry
  3½ yards very light topaz
  10½ yards pale delft
  3½ yards light Nile green
- #3 pearl cotton:
  ½ yard snow white
  1 yard light lavender
  2 yards light cranberry
  2 yards light Nile green
- ¹⁄₁₆"-wide double-faced satin ribbon:
  2¼ yards white
  6" orchid
  8" light blue
  2 yards mint
  3 yards pink
- Small bugle beads: 1 package each white and pink
- Frosted glass beads: 1 package each white, pink, green and yellow
- White sewing thread and needle
- Hot-glue gun

Instructions

1. Cut plastic canvas according to graphs (also see Page 46).

2. With #5 pearl cotton, Cross Stitch backgrounds following individual graphs for colors and Fig. 1 as a stitching sample. Backgrounds for Eggs 1–3 are stitched with two colors; backgrounds for Eggs 4–6 are stitched with variegated (or shaded) yarn; and backgrounds for Eggs 7–9 are stitched with a solid color. Overcast eggs with adjacent colors.

3. After background stitching is complete, embroider eggs in the following order:

- Work all Fly Stitch, Lazy Daisy and Long Stitches.
- Work all couching and ribbon Lazy Daisy stitching.
- Work all Backstitching
- Work all French Knots
- Using white thread, work all beading.

4. For Egg 4, weave ribbon Long Stitches over Cross Stitches. For Egg 7, weave ribbon where vertical and horizontal Long Stitches cross.

5. Cut nine 5" lengths of white dou-ble-faced satin ribbon. Make hanging loops, bringing ribbon through stitching on back of eggs. Tie ends in a knot and glue to secure. ❖

Easter Eggs
15 holes x 24 holes
Cut 1 each

Fig. 1

COLOR KEYS
Color numbers given are for DMC #5 and #3 pearl cotton, Wrights 1⁄16" double-faced satin ribbon and Mill Hill frosted glass and bugle beads.

EGG 1
#5 Pearl Cotton
Uncoded areas are snow white
Cross Stitches
▨ Pale delft #800
#3 Pearl Cotton
● Light cranberry #603 French Knot
○ Light Nile green #955 French Knot
Frosted Glass Beads
○ Pink #62035
● Green #62038
Bugle Beads
▨ Pink #72035

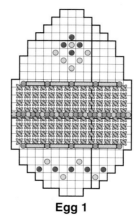

Egg 1

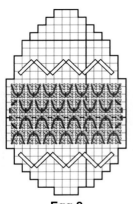

Egg 2

EGG 2

#5 Pearl Cotton

Uncoded areas are very light
topaz #727 Cross Stitches

▨ Light Nile green #955

#3 Pearl Cotton

ⱱ Snow white Fly Stitch

╱ Snow white Backstitch

ⱱ Light cranberry #603 Fly Stitch

Bugle Beads

▭ White #70479

Egg 6

EGG 6

#5 Pearl Cotton

Uncoded background is shaded
yellows #90 Cross Stitches

ⱱ Snow white Fly Stitch

#3 Pearl Cotton

╱ Light lavender #210 Backstitch

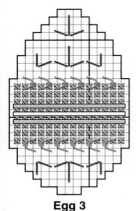

Egg 3

EGG 3

#5 Pearl Cotton

Uncoded areas are very light
cranberry #604 Cross Stitches

▨ Light lavender #210

#3 Pearl Cotton

╱ Snow white Backstitch

ⱱ Light Nile green #955 Fly Stitch

¹⁄₁₆" Double-Faced Satin Ribbon

▭ White #030 Straight Stitch

▭ Pink #061 Straight Stitch

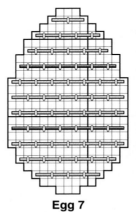

Egg 7

EGG 7

#5 Pearl Cotton

Uncoded area is snow
white Cross Stitches

☐ Snow white (used to couch ribbon)

¹⁄₁₆" Double-Faced Satin Ribbon

▬ Orchid #051 Couching

▭ Light blue #052 Couching

▭ Mint #056 Couching

▭ Pink #061 Couching

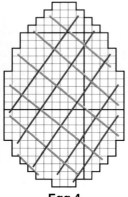

Egg 4

EGG 4

#5 Pearl Cotton

Uncoded background is shaded
roses #48 Cross Stitches

¹⁄₁₆" Double-Faced Satin Ribbon

╱ Mint #056 Long Stitch

╱ Pink #061 Long Stitch

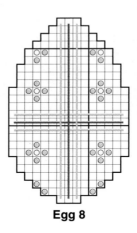

Egg 8

EGG 8

#5 Pearl Cotton

Uncoded area is light
lavender #210 Cross Stitches

¹⁄₁₆" Double-Faced Satin Ribbon

○ White #030 French Knot

╱ White #030 Long Stitch

╱ Mint #056 Long Stitch

● Pink #061 French Knot

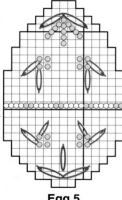

Egg 5

EGG 5

#5 Pearl Cotton

Uncoded background is shaded
bright greens #101 Cross Stitches

¹⁄₁₆" Double-Faced Satin Ribbon

❖ White #030 Lazy Daisy

❖ Pink #061 Lazy Daisy

Frosted Glass Beads

○ White #60479

● Yellow #62041

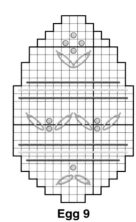

Egg 9

EGG 9

#5 Pearl Cotton

Uncoded area is pale
delft #800 Cross Stitches

¹⁄₁₆" Double-Faced Satin Ribbon

╱ White #030 Long Stitch

❖ Mint #056 Lazy Daisy

● Pink #061 French Knot

╱ Pink #061 Long Stitch

Jelly Bean Bunnies
Continued from Page 43

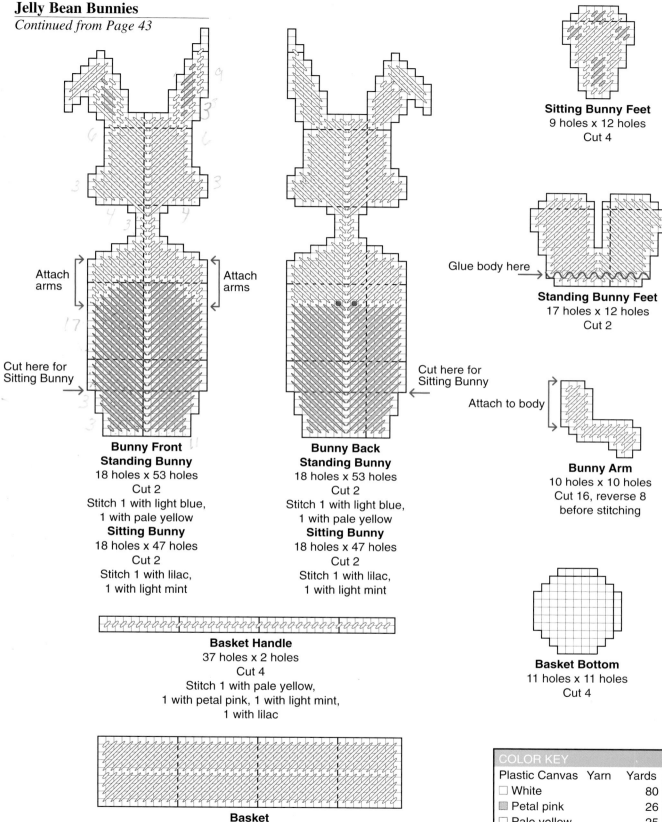

Sitting Bunny Feet
9 holes x 12 holes
Cut 4

Glue body here →

Standing Bunny Feet
17 holes x 12 holes
Cut 2

Attach to body

Bunny Arm
10 holes x 10 holes
Cut 16, reverse 8
before stitching

Attach arms

Attach arms

Cut here for
Sitting Bunny →

← Cut here for
Sitting Bunny

Bunny Front
Standing Bunny
18 holes x 53 holes
Cut 2
Stitch 1 with light blue,
1 with pale yellow
Sitting Bunny
18 holes x 47 holes
Cut 2
Stitch 1 with lilac,
1 with light mint

Bunny Back
Standing Bunny
18 holes x 53 holes
Cut 2
Stitch 1 with light blue,
1 with pale yellow
Sitting Bunny
18 holes x 47 holes
Cut 2
Stitch 1 with lilac,
1 with light mint

Basket Bottom
11 holes x 11 holes
Cut 4

Basket Handle
37 holes x 2 holes
Cut 4
Stitch 1 with pale yellow,
1 with petal pink, 1 with light mint,
1 with lilac

Basket
38 holes x 9 holes
Cut 4
Stitch 1 with pale yellow,
1 with petal pink, 1 with light mint,
1 with lilac

COLOR KEY		
Plastic Canvas	Yarn	Yards
☐ White		80
▨ Petal pink		26
☐ Pale yellow		25
▨ Light blue		15
Light mint		25
Lilac		25
● Overall strap placement		

47

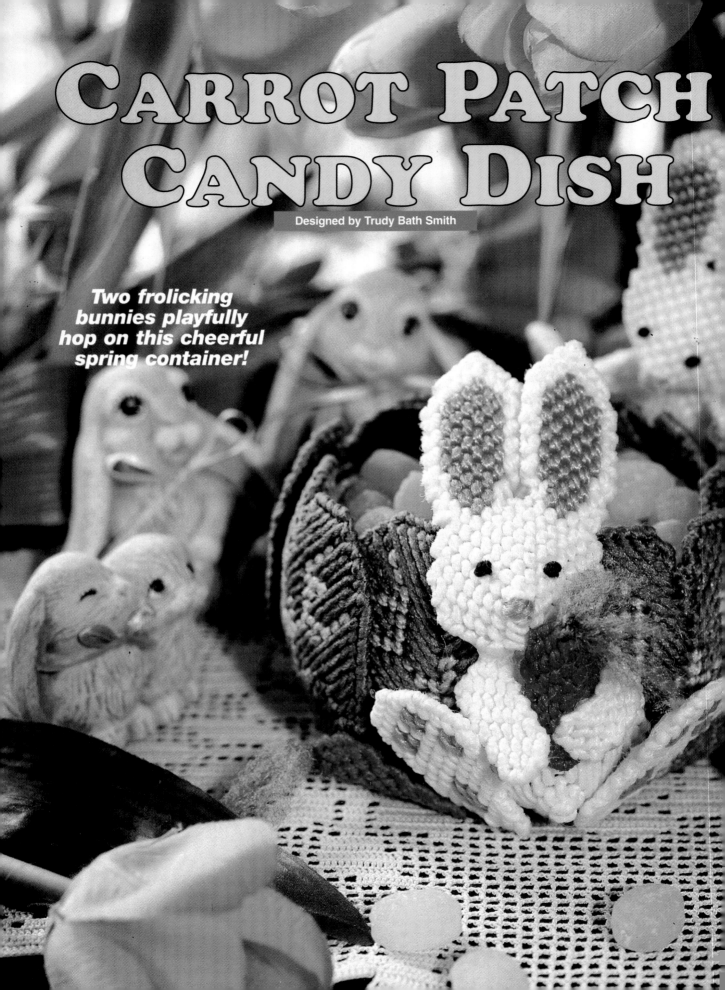

CARROT PATCH CANDY DISH

Designed by Trudy Bath Smith

Two frolicking bunnies playfully hop on this cheerful spring container!

Skill Level: Beginner

Materials

- 2½ sheets 7-count plastic canvas
- 4½ " plastic canvas circle
- ⅓ sheet light green 7-count plastic canvas
- Plastic canvas yarn as listed in color key
- Hot-glue gun
- 8-ounce soft margarine tub, empty (optional)

Instructions

1. Cut plastic canvas according to graphs (Page 50). Cut one 90-hole x 14-hole piece from light green plastic canvas for liner.

2. Stitch pieces following graphs. Overcast bunny paws with white. With bittersweet, Overcast carrots and Whipstitch dart together. Cut two 3" lengths of Christmas green. Stitch one length through top of each carrot at dart, so that both ends stick up at top of carrot. Tie in a knot and spread yarn slightly. Set aside.

3. With moss, Whipstitch short edges of liner together, overlapping 3 holes. Overcast liner top edge with moss.

4. Overcast all cabbage leaf edges except bottom edge with avocado. Whipstitch three darts on leaves together with avocado. With avocado, Whipstitch leaf bottoms to circle bottom edge, spacing evenly and Overcasting circle edge between leaves.

5. Glue bottom edge of liner to inside circle. Holding leaves up, glue to top edge of liner, overlapping while gluing.

Sitting Bunny

1. With white, Overcast bottom edge of sitting bunny's ear back, then Whipstitch ears to head front. With white, Overcast remaining edges of head front, Whipstitching bottom dart together. Whipstitch two times with powder pink at top of dart for nose.

2. With white, Overcast one body front, Whipstitching bottom dart together. Whipstitch paws to body where indicated on graph. Overcast two foot bottoms with white. Using photo as a guide, glue wrong side of foot bottoms to bottom of bunny body.

3. Using photo as a guide, glue wrong side of sitting bunny's body to candy dish so that bottom edges are nearly even, then glue head to top of body. Glue carrot to front of body, then glue one paw around carrot. Glue remaining carrot to side of bunny at bottom of dish.

Climbing Bunny

1. With white, Whipstitch bottom dart of head back together. Repeat for head front, Whipstitching two times with powder pink at top of dart for nose. Overcast bottom edges of head pieces with white. Whipstitch remaining edges of head front and back together with white.

2. With white, Whipstitch bottom dart on body front together. Repeat for body back, adding four to five Turkey Loops to top of dart for tail. Clip loops and fluff, trimming as needed.

3. With white, Whipstitch body front to body back, then Whipstitch paws to body sides where indicated on graph.

4. With wrong sides together, Whipstitch bunny foot bottoms to bunny foot tops. Glue tops of feet to body front. Insert top of body into head bottom and glue to attach.

5. Using photo as a guide, glue front of bunny to cabbage dish so he appears to be peeking over top edge of dish.

6. If desired, insert empty margarine tub into cabbage dish and fill with candy. ❖

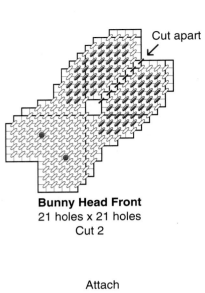

Bunny Head Front
21 holes x 21 holes
Cut 2

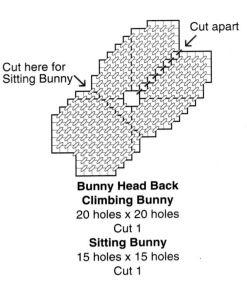

Bunny Head Back
Climbing Bunny
20 holes x 20 holes
Cut 1
Sitting Bunny
15 holes x 15 holes
Cut 1

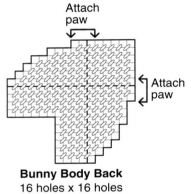

Bunny Body Back
16 holes x 16 holes
Cut 1

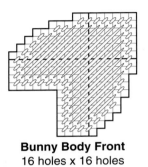

Bunny Body Front
16 holes x 16 holes
Cut 2

Bunny Foot Bottom
12 holes x 12 holes
Cut 4

Bunny Foot Top
12 holes x 12 holes
Cut 2

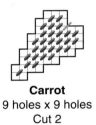

Carrot
9 holes x 9 holes
Cut 2

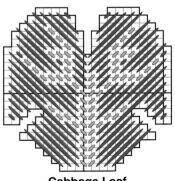

Cabbage Leaf
21 holes x 21 holes
Cut 7

Bunny Paw
8 holes x 8 holes
Cut 4

COLOR KEY	
Plastic Canvas Yarn	**Yards**
☐ White #01	45
▨ Powder pink #11	7
■ Bittersweet #18	3
▨ Avocado #30	27
☐ Moss #48	15
╱ Christmas green #58 (carrot leaf)	¼
● Royal dark blue #07 French Knot	1
Color numbers given are for Darice Nylon Plus plastic canvas yarn.	

50

ADD A LITTLE SPARKLE!

Learn how to add a little sparkle to your stitching with little time and effort!

By Vicki Blizzard

Did you ever wish for an easy way to add rhinestones and metal studs to your plastic canvas work? I know I did. I love the look of sparkling accents on my stitching, but am easily frustrated by burning my fingers while trying to hot-glue them in place.

I've tried using thinner jewel glues, but don't like the look of the glue around the outside edges of the rhinestone (which is what most labels recommend); and I also don't have the patience to let the piece dry flat for several hours, which means my rhinestones often end up in different spots than where I placed them!

I have found a wonderful product which applies many different sizes and types of rhinestones, pearls and metal studs on fabric, stitching, wood, glass—just about any surface you can think of! The product is a BeJeweler™ rhinestone setter by Creative Crystal Co.

The BeJeweler is a tool that resembles an electric wood-burning tool in that it has a handle and a changeable metal tip which heats up quickly to a very high temperature.

The rhinestones manufactured by Creative Crystal Co. are Austrian crystal rhinestones with a special heat-activated adhesive applied to the backs. Heat-set pearls and metal studs in copper, silver and gold are also available.

After the tool is plugged in and the appropriate tip is heated (this takes only a few minutes), a round rhinestone is picked up with the tip, and the hot tip melts the adhesive in a matter of seconds. The tool is then held perpendicular to the surface and the rhinestone placed exactly where you want it. Pull the tool away, and the rhinestone is permanently glued in place. No more burned fingers or misplaced rhinestones!

To apply novelty-shaped rhinestones such as teardrops or flowers, a Hot Spot tip is used. The rhinestone is placed where desired, and the tip is touched to the front of the rhinestone. The adhesive then melts and bonds the rhinestone in place. Metal studs are also applied in this manner.

The BeJeweler Kit includes a size 16ss (4mm) tip, support stand, sample rhinestones, warranty card and very clear directions. It retails for $34.95. Several other tips are available to apply other sizes and shapes of rhinestones and studs.

The rhinestones are a very high-quality Austrian crystal, and are more expensive than traditional acrylic rhinestones; but once you see the quality, I hope you'll agree that they're well worth the extra cost. They are available in a wide variety of sizes, shapes and colors. Half-round pearls and metal studs in 13 styles are also available.

Imagine the uses of this product! Stitched plastic canvas can be decorated with jewels and pearls in no time at all. Rhinestones, studs and pearls can be applied as a decorative accent to painted T-shirts (yes—the jewels and studs are washable and dry-cleanable and will not tarnish or discolor). Or how about using the tool to apply rhinestones to handmade jewelry? The possibilities are endless!

For ordering information, contact Creative Crystal Co., P.O. Box 8, Unionville, CT

TRIBUTE TO MOM & DAD

Express your love to your parents this year by making any of the wonderful gift ideas included in this attractive chapter. You'll find pretty and practical gifts for Mom such as a gift box planter and sparkling earrings. And what father wouldn't enjoy being told he's the world's greatest dad with an antique car keeper or a handsome desk organizer?

WORLD'S GREATEST

Designed by Mary T. Cosgrove

Make your dad feel No. 1 with this special Father's Day tissue box cover insert. Stitch it in his favorite colors or to match his office!

DAD

Skill Level: Beginner

Materials

- ¼ sheet 7-count plastic canvas
- Plastic canvas yarn as listed in color key
- 1½ yards white/silver plastic canvas cord
- Lucite boutique tissue box cover

Instructions

1. Cut plastic canvas according to graph.

2. Continental, Gobelin and Cross Stitch piece following graph.

3. Overcast edges with white/silver cord.

4. Insert plastic canvas into front of Lucite boutique box. ❖

COLOR KEY	
Plastic Canvas Yarn	**Yards**
■ Fern #23	5
■ Royal #32	8
☐ White #41	5
Color numbers given are for Uniek Needloft plastic canvas yarn.	

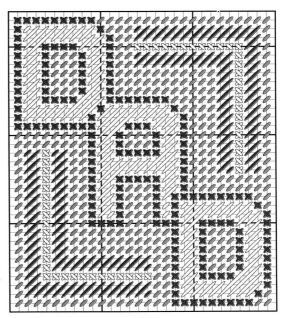

Insert
29 holes x 34 holes
Cut 1

SONGBIRD

Designed by Dianne Davis

Perched on her stoop, this lovely songbird sings to her heart's content. Hung in a bright sunny window, this pretty project will bring a smile to your face year-round.

Skill Level: Beginner

Materials

- 1 sheet ivory 7-count plastic canvas
- Plastic canvas yarn as listed in color key
- #16 or #18 tapestry needle
- 3" bird (sample used a wren)
- Small amount Spanish moss
- Small silk flowers and leaves to coordinate with bird (sample used coral, blue and white)
- 3¼" square black self-adhesive felt
- 18" ⅛"-wide double-faced satin ribbon to coordinate with bird (sample used peach)
- Fishing line or clear plastic thread
- Craft glue

Instructions

1. Cut plastic canvas according to graphs. Cut one 24-hole x 24-hole square for birdhouse back. Back will remain unstitched.

2. Stitch pieces following graphs, Overcasting platform, brace and inside edges of front opening with natural.

3. Using fishing line or clear plastic thread, attach brace to platform where indicated on graph. Attach both brace and platform to front piece where indicated on graph with fishing line or clear plastic thread.

4. With natural, Whipstitch sides to front, then Whipstitch edges of lower corner.

5. With sage, Whipstitch roof pieces where indicated on graph to top front edges of birdhouse. With sage, Whipstitch short edges of roof and birdhouse sides together, then remaining short roof edges together at top of roof. Overcast edges of roof overhang with sage. Attach hanger with sage yarn to rear point of roof.

6. Center and attach felt to unstitched back piece. With sage, Whipstitch roof to back piece with felt on inside of birdhouse. With ivory, Whipstitch sides to back.

7. Place Spanish moss into bottom of birdhouse, until even with opening. Using photo as a guide, glue small mount of Spanish moss to platform.

8. Glue bird to Spanish moss and platform. Arrange and glue flowers and leaves to Spanish moss around and behind bird.

9. Tie ribbon in a bow and glue to front point of roof. Twist ends of ribbon slightly and glue to roof in desired position. ❖

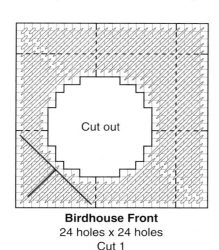

Birdhouse Front
24 holes x 24 holes
Cut 1

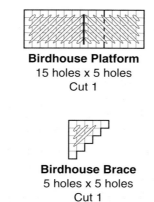

Birdhouse Platform
15 holes x 5 holes
Cut 1

Birdhouse Brace
5 holes x 5 holes
Cut 1

COLOR KEY	
Plastic Canvas Yarn	**Yards**
☐ Natural #0002	15
■ Sage #0050	13
╱ Attach brace	
╱ Attach platform and brace	

Color numbers given are for Spinrite plastic canvas yarn.

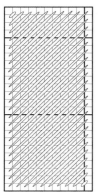

Birdhouse Left Side
11 holes x 24 holes
Cut 1

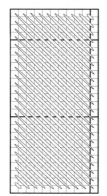

Birdhouse Right Side
11 holes x 24 holes
Cut 1

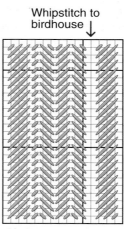

Whipstitch to birdhouse ↓

Birdhouse Left Roof
15 holes x 24 holes
Cut 1

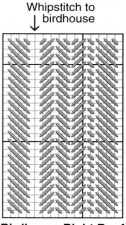

Whipstitch to birdhouse ↓

Birdhouse Right Roof
15 holes x 24 holes
Cut 1

PLAID DESK ORG

Designed by Joan Green

Keep your bills, letters, coupons and other odds and ends at your fingertips in this attractive desk organizer. It makes a perfect gift for a man or a woman.

Skill Level: Intermediate

Materials

- 1½ sheets stiff 7-count plastic canvas
- Plastic canvas yarn as listed in color key
- Metallic #7 plastic canvas yarn as listed in color key
- #16 tapestry needle
- Self-adhesive white felt

Instructions

1. Cut plastic canvas according to graphs (also see next page). Cut one 65-hole x 29-hole piece for organizer base.

2. Continental Stitch front and side pieces following graphs. Stitch fleur de lis pattern on back piece with gold metallic yarn; fill in background with wine Gobelin Stitches. Gobelin Stitch dividers with navy.

3. Overcast side and top edges of dividers with navy. Overcast top edges of back, front and side pieces with wine.

4. With wine, Whipstitch together right side of back to wrong side of sides, then Whipstitch together wrong sides of front to wrong sides of sides. With wine, Whipstitch organizer to unstitched base.

5. Aligning one divider with center vertical row of navy on sides and the remaining divider with the back vertical navy row, tack each piece at three points on each side, working over navy stitches to conceal stitching. With navy, tack to box base in center of each divider.

6. Cut felt to line wrong side of back piece and underneath side of base and attach. ❖

COLOR KEY	
Plastic Canvas Yarn	**Yards**
■ Wine #0011	55
■ Poplar #0051	20
■ Navy #0068	55
Metallic Plastic Canvas Yarn	
☐ Yellow gold #PC7	2
Color numbers given are for Darice Nylon Plus plastic canvas yarn and Rainbow Gallery Metallic #7 plastic canvas yarn.	

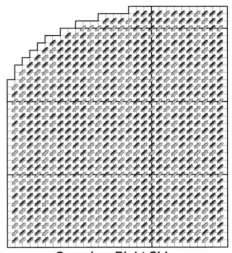

Organizer Right Side
29 holes x 33 holes
Cut 1

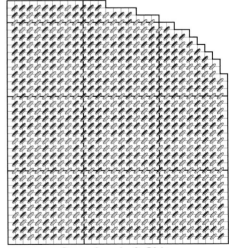

Organizer Left Side
29 holes x 33 holes
Cut 1

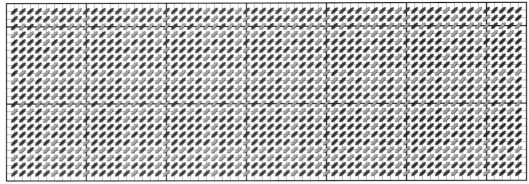

Organizer Front
65 holes x 23 holes
Cut 1

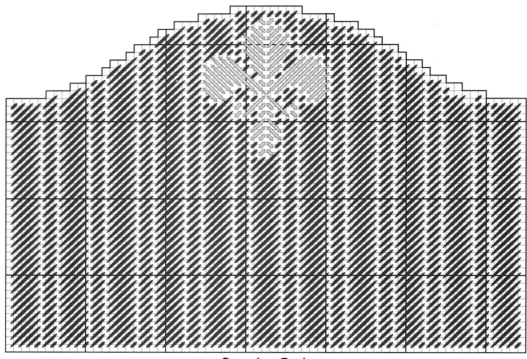

Organizer Back
65 holes x 45 holes
Cut 1

Organizer Divider
64 holes x 30 holes
Cut 2

Shimmery Blue Earrings

Designed by Linda Wyszynski

Stitch up a pair of these sparkly earrings for a special gift or special occasion! One pair can be completed in just an hour!

Skill Level: Beginner

Materials

- ¼ sheet 10-count plastic canvas
- Variegated sport weight cotton yarn as listed in color key
- Medium (#16) metallic braid as listed in color key
- 1 yard 6-strand embroidery floss: light cornflower blue
- 30 blue seed beads
- 2 gold French ear wires
- 2 small gold jump rings
- 2 medium gold jump rings • Beading needle
- #24 tapestry needle
- Needle-nose pliers

Instructions

1. Cut plastic canvas according to graphs.

2. Stitch earring fronts and backs following graphs, using 2 strands twilight. When Straight Stitching with medium (#16) braid, keep braid flat by guiding it between thumb and forefinger of free hand and dropping needle occasionally to let braid unwind.

3. Using 2 strands embroidery floss, attach beads where indicated on graph, sewing through each bead twice to secure.

4. With wrong sides together, Whipstitch a front and back piece together with 2 strands twilight. Repeat for other earring.

5. Using needle-nose pliers, carefully work small jump ring into center top of each earring as indicated on graph. Secure a medium jump ring to small ring. Secure French ear wire to medium jump ring. ❖

COLOR KEY	
Cotton Yarn	**Yards**
▪ Twilight	3
Medium (#16) Braid	
╱ Sky blue #014HL Straight Stitch	1½
● Attach seed beads blue #794	
Color numbers given are for Kreinik Medium (#16) braid and Mill Hill seed beads. Twilight Watercolours cotton yarn from The Caron Collection.	

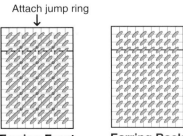

Attach jump ring

Earring Front
9 holes x 13 holes
Cut 2

Earring Back
9 holes x 13 holes
Cut 2

CLASSIC CAR KEEPER

Designed by Karen McDanel

Please an antique car enthusiast with this striking keeper. The roof opens up to reveal a storage place inside perfect for keeping coins, notes, tie tacks or other odds & ends.

Skill Level: Advanced

Materials

- 2 sheets 7-count plastic canvas
- 14 (3") plastic canvas circles
- 4-ply worsted weight yarn as listed in color key
- Metallic cord as listed in color key
- Hot-glue gun

Instructions

1. Cut plastic canvas according to graphs (Pages 64 and 65). Cut one 58-hole x 25-hole piece for car bottom and 12 (3-hole x 3-hole) pieces for bumper supports. Bottom and bumper supports will remain unstitched.

2. Stitch pieces following graphs. Backstitch with 2 plies nickel over forest green stitches. For wheels, place two circles together and stitch through both thicknesses. Repeat

for remaining four wheels.

3. Overcast front and back bumpers, headlights and taillights with silver. Overcast two long sides and one short side of each fender with forest green. Place three unstitched bumper supports together and Whipstitch around edges with forest green. Repeat for remaining supports.

4. With black, Whipstitch one running board to unstitched short edges of one front and back fender. Repeat for remaining running board and fenders. With black, Whipstitch bottom piece to car sides where indicated on graph.

5. With black, Whipstitch one running board to bottom and side of car. Repeat for remaining running board. Overcast remaining unworked edges of running boards with black.

6. With forest green, Whipstitch

windshield to hood and hood to front. With black, Whipstitch front to bottom. With forest green, Whipstitch back window to trunk. Whipstitch trunk to bottom with black. Whipstitch assembled pieces to car sides with forest green.

7. With forest green, Overcast unstitched top edges of sides and windshield. Overcast front and side edges of top with forest green. Whipstitch back edge of top to back window with forest green.

8. Glue bumper supports to lower corners on front and back fenders. Glue front and back bumpers to supports.

9. Using photo as a guide, glue four wheels in place under fenders. Glue fifth wheel to trunk above handle, taillights to back under fenders and above bumpers and headlights to front. ❖

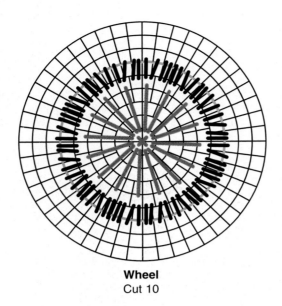

Wheel
Cut 10

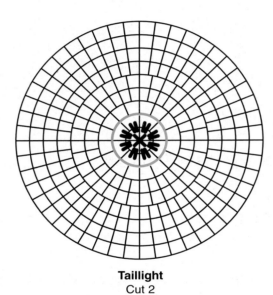

Taillight
Cut 2

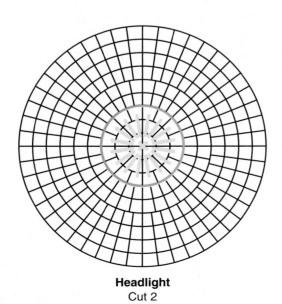

Headlight
Cut 2

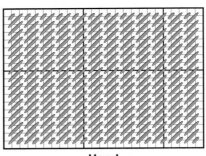

Hood
25 holes x 18 holes
Cut 1

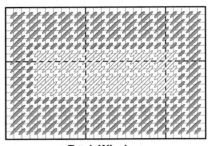

Back Window
25 holes x 17 holes
Cut 1

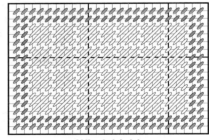

Windshield
25 holes x 17 holes
Cut 1

Back Edge

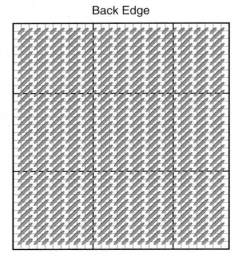

Top
27 holes x 29 holes
Cut 1

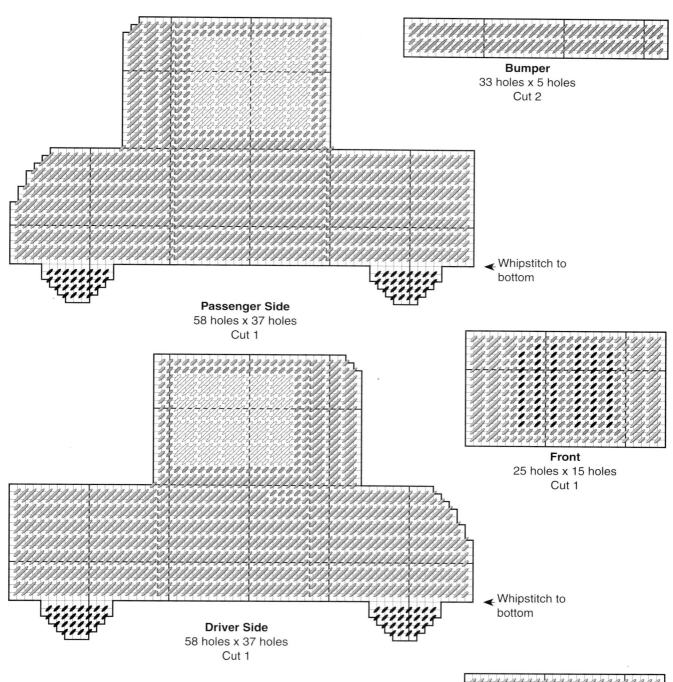

Bumper
33 holes x 5 holes
Cut 2

Passenger Side
58 holes x 37 holes
Cut 1

◄ Whipstitch to bottom

Front
25 holes x 15 holes
Cut 1

Driver Side
58 holes x 37 holes
Cut 1

◄ Whipstitch to bottom

COLOR KEY	
4-Ply Worsted Weight Yarn	**Yards**
▨ Forest green #689	85
☐ White #1	11
■ Black #12	20
▨ Warm brown #336	5
■ **Jockey red #902**	**1**
☐ Yellow #230	1
– Nickel #401 Backstitch	3
Metallic Cord	
▨ Silver #3411-02	18

Color numbers given are for Red Heart 4-ply worsted weight yarn by Coats & Clark and Darice Bright Jewels Metallic Cord.

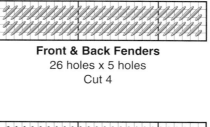

Front & Back Fenders
26 holes x 5 holes
Cut 4

Running Board
26 holes x 5 holes
Cut 2

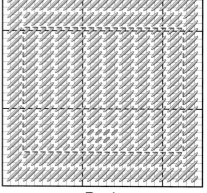

Trunk
25 holes x 25 holes
Cut 1

World's Best Mom

Designed by Karen McDanel

Delight your mother with this pretty floral mug singing her praises. She's sure to think of you every time she uses it!

Skill Level: Beginner

Materials

- 1/3 sheet 10-count plastic canvas
- 3-ply sport weight yarn as listed in color key
- Cream-rimmed plastic mug with insert area

Instructions

1. Cut plastic canvas according to graph.

2. Stitch piece following graph. With off-white, Overcast long edges. Whipstitch short edges together with off-white.

3. Place mug insert inside mug with joined edges at center back.

4. Remove insert before washing mug. ❖

COLOR KEY	
3-Ply Sport Weight Yarn	**Yards**
■ Burgundy	9
▨ Tropical pink	9
▩ Green	7
☐ Off-white	31

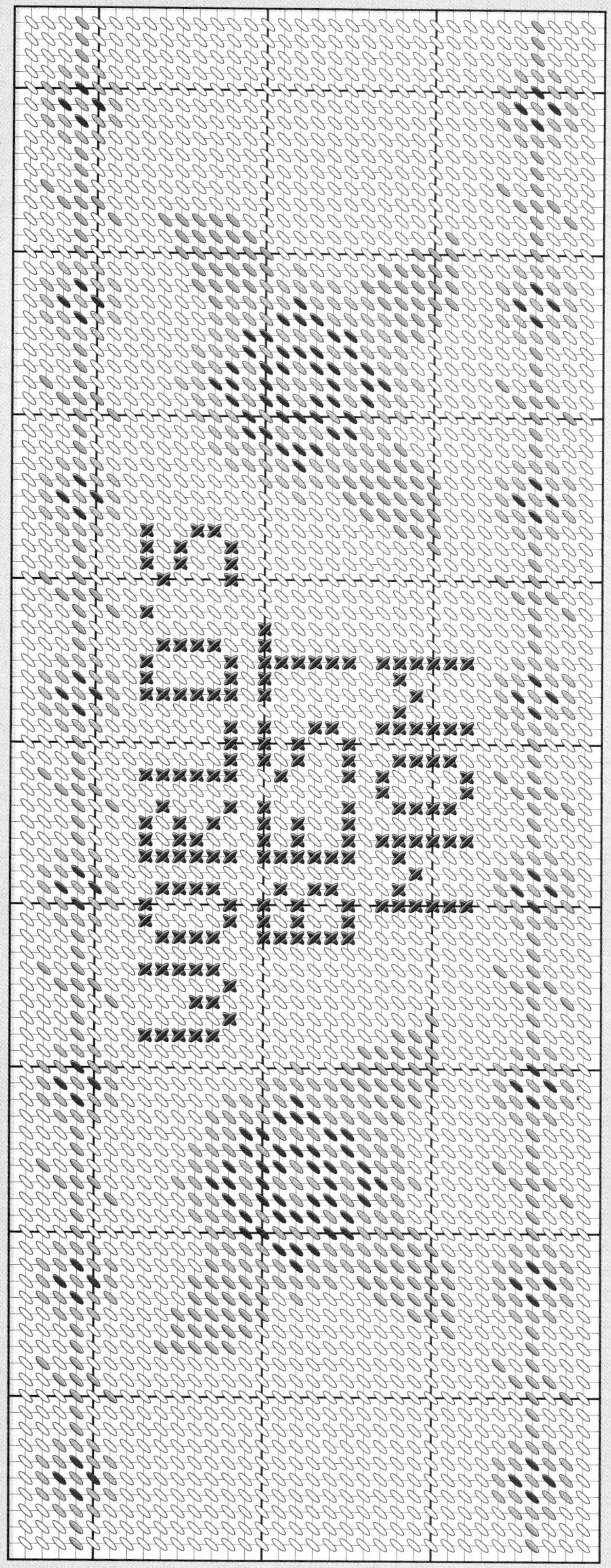

Mug Insert
95 holes x 35 holes
Cut 1

GIFT BOX PLANTER

Designed by Lois Winston

This pretty plant pot cover makes a wonderful gift for Mother's Day! Choose a blooming plant with flowers to match the bow

Skill Level: Beginner

Materials

- 3 sheets stiff 7-count plastic canvas
- 1 sheet soft 7-count plastic canvas
- 4-ply yarn as listed in color key
- ¾" pink ceramic heart button
- Sewing needle and pink thread
- Low-temp glue gun

Instructions

1. Cut side pieces from ultra-stiff plastic canvas and bow loops from soft plastic canvas according to graphs. Cut one 42-hole x 42-hole piece for box bottom.

2. Stitch pieces following graphs. Box bottom will remain unstitched.

3. Overcast long edges of bow loops with dark jade. With dark jade, Whipstitch short edges of one loop together. Repeat for remaining three loops.

4. With cream, Overcast top edges of sides. With cream, Whipstitch box sides together and then sides to bottom.

5. With seam at back center and using pink thread, attach button to one bow loop, sewing through both thicknesses. Glue second loop to itself at inside center with seam at back center. Repeat with remaining two loops.

6. Glue one loop vertically to box, centered over stitched ribbon stripe. Glue second loop diagonally over first loop, then third loop diagonally in opposite direction over second loop. Glue loop with button horizontally over third loop. Tack ends of diagonal loops to box. ❖

COLOR KEY

4-Ply Yarn
- ▧ Dark jade
- ▨ Rose
- ☐ Cream

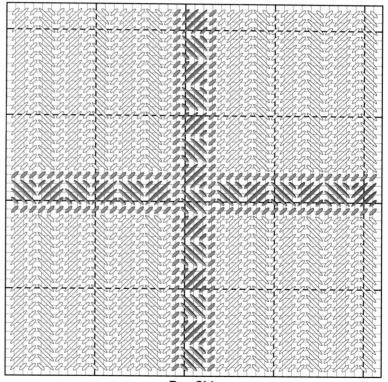

Box Side
42 holes x 43 holes
Cut 4 from stiff

Bow Loop
73 holes x 4 holes
Cut 4 from soft

GOLDEN DIAMONDS GIFT BOX

Designed by Kathy Wirth

Delight your mother with this unusual hexagon-shaped gift box. Fabric yo-yos and gold braid add a special touch!

Skill Level: Beginner

Materials

- 2 (5") plastic canvas hexagons
- ½ sheet clear 7-count plastic canvas
- Plastic canvas yarn as listed in color key
- ⅛" gold metallic braid as listed in color key
- 6 small (approximately 1") pastel fabric yo-yos
- 14mm round gold bead
- 6 (6mm) round gold beads
- ½ sheet white self-adhesive felt
- 2 yards fine gold braid
- 1 skein white 6-strand embroidery floss
- #18 and #24 tapestry needles
- Pencil

Instructions

1. Place unworked hexagon shape on wrong side of felt. Use pencil to mark through each hole of outer row. Cut along pencil line.

2. Cut sides according to graph. From regular sheet of plastic canvas, cut six 16-hole x 4-hole pieces for lid lips.

3. Continental Stitch sides and lid according to graphs. Add gold braid outlines as indicated on graphs.

4. Whipstitch short ends of lid lips together with 12 strands of white floss to form a circle.

5. Use green plastic canvas yarn to Whipstitch lips to lid through first and third row of holes on outer edges around entire lid. Form an X at each of the corners. To avoid distortion, skip one hole in the center of each lip piece. With ⅛" gold braid, Overcast lid through second row of holes on outer edges.

6. With fine gold braid and using #24 tapestry needle, attach one yo-yo and one small gold bead to the center of each side.

7. Whipstitch sides together in pairs with lilac yarn. Whipstitch pairs together with green yarn, forming circle.

8. Whipstitch sides to bottom and Overcast top edge of box with ⅛" gold braid.

9. Sew large gold bead to lid center with ⅛" braid. Place felt liner in box bottom. ❖

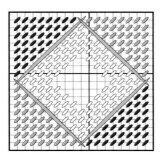

Box Side
18 holes x 18 holes
Cut 6

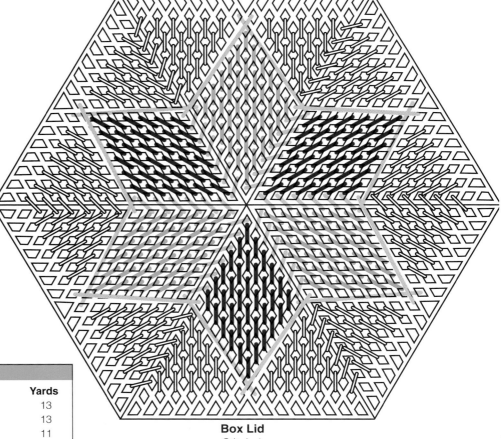

Box Lid
Stitch 1

COLOR KEY	
Plastic Canvas Yarn	**Yards**
☐ White #0101	13
▦ Apple green #0145	13
▦ Lilac #0148	11
⅛" Metallic Braid	
▦ Gold #01	8½
— Gold #01 Straight Stitch	
Color numbers given are for Bernat Cotton Plastic Canvas Yarn and GlissenGloss Braid Plus Four.	

SALUTE TO AMERICA

Demonstrate your pride in America by decorating your home in red, white and blue. From a cheerful picnic set to sparkling stars-and-stripes jewelry, this chapter is bursting with ways to express your American patriotism.

SUMMER PICNIC

Designed by Nancy Marshall

Whether for the annual Fourth of July family reunion or for any outdoor summer picnic, this red, white and blue raffia ribbon set is perfect for the occasion!

Skill Level: Beginner

Materials

- 1 sheet 7-count stiff plastic canvas
- 3¼ sheets 7-count plastic canvas
- 1 (10-yard) package each color raffia ribbon as listed in color key
- Clear tape

Project Notes

When cutting raffia ribbon, wrap tape around both ends. Measure 18" from end of ribbon, wrap tape around ribbon at this point. Cut through middle of tape.

When stitching with raffia ribbon, be careful to keep ribbon flat. Ribbon may be held flat by holding between thumb and forefinger of the free hand to help guide it.

Instructions

1. Cut plastic canvas according to graphs (Pages 76 and 77). Cut one 57-hole x 33-hole piece for large box bottom and one 25-hole x 7-hole piece for coaster box bottom.

Box bottoms will remain un-stitched.

2. Stitch pieces following graphs. For place mat, stitch checkerboard and stripe patterns before Back-stitching with red. Overcast edges with red.

3. For large box, Overcast top edges of front, back and sides with red. With ribbon matching color of front and back pieces, Whipstitch sides to front and back pieces so stripe colors alternate all around. Whipstitch large box bottom to sides with adjacent colors.

4. For napkin ring, Overcast long edges with red. Whipstitch short ends together with blue.

5. For coasters, Overcast edges with adjacent colors. For coaster box, Overcast top edges of front, back and sides with adjacent colors. With ribbon matching color of front and back pieces, Whipstitch sides to front and back pieces so stripe colors alternate all around. Whipstitch coaster box bottom to sides with adjacent colors. ❖

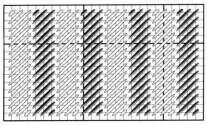

Coaster Box Front & Back
25 holes x 15 holes
Cut 2

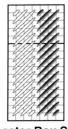

Coaster Box Side
7 holes x 15 holes
Cut 2

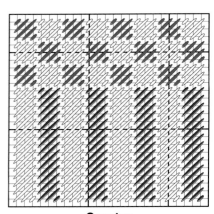

Coaster
25 holes x 25 holes
Cut 4

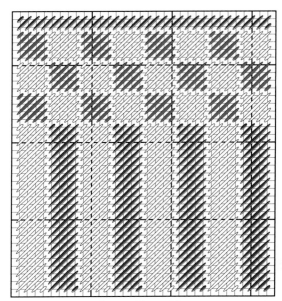

Large Box Side
33 holes x 37 holes
Cut 2

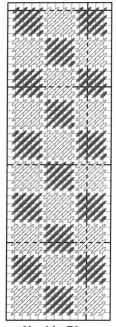

Napkin Ring
13 holes x 41 holes
Cut 1

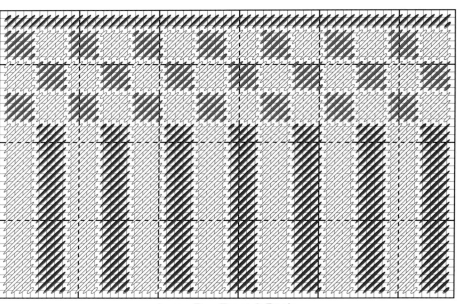

Large Box Front & Back
57 holes x 37 holes
Cut 2

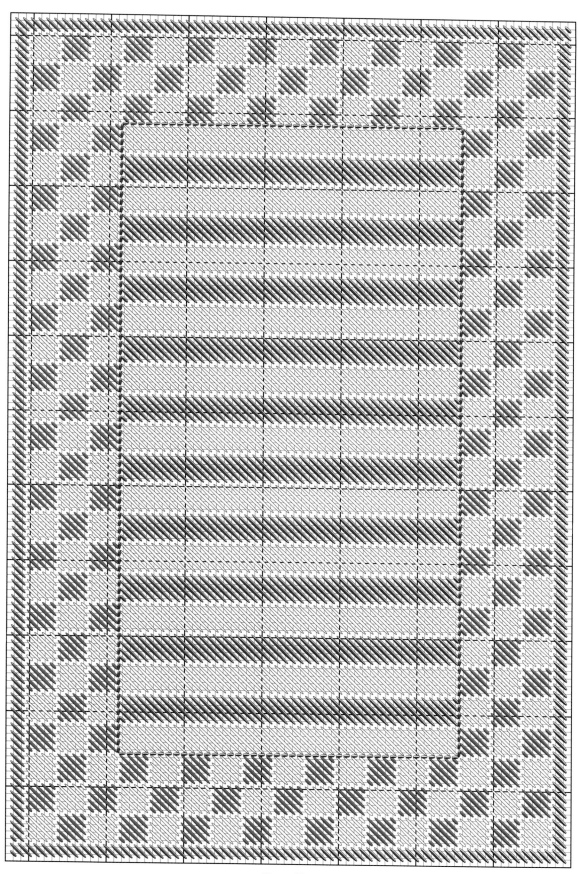

Place Mat
113 holes x 73 holes
Cut 1

UNCLE SAM'S BANK

Designed by Michele Wilcox

Encourage your youngsters to save with this cheerful bank! Decorated with sparkling white stars and a watchful Uncle Sam, saving money in this bank is old-fashioned fun!

Skill Level: Beginner

Materials

- 1 sheet clear 7-count plastic canvas
- Plastic canvas yarn as listed in color key
- Hot-glue gun
- 12" ¼" wooden dowel (for cake topper only)

Bank

1. Cut plastic canvas according to graphs.

2. Stitch according to graphs, using Continental Stitches and Slanting Gobelin Stitches. Following graph, stitch two French Knots with royal for eyes and one French Knot with red for mouth.

3. Overcast Uncle Sam as follows: Overcast beard and mustache with white, top of hat with royal, hatband with white and hat brim with royal. Glue mustache onto head using photo as a guide.

4. Overcast coin slot opening with red. Whipstitch bank top, sides and bottom together with royal. Overcast bottom edges with royal.

5. Glue Uncle Sam to bank at top left-hand corner at a slight angle.

6. To remove money from bank, use a butter knife to enlarge size of opening. **Note:** *For ease in removing money, we suggest that you do not place paper money in bank, only coins.* ❖

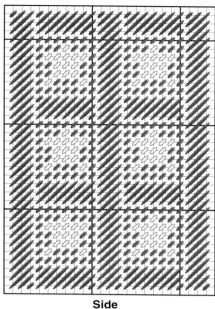

Side
24 holes x 34 holes
Cut 4

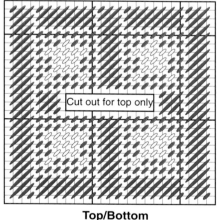

Top/Bottom
24 holes x 24 holes
Cut 2

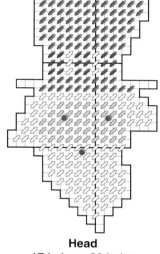

Head
17 holes x 28 holes
Cut 1

Mustache
7 holes x 3 holes
Cut 1

COLOR KEY	
Plastic Canvas Yarn	**Yards**
■ Red #01	36
□ White #41	18
■ Royal #32	33
▨ Fleshtone #56	2
● Royal #32 French Knot	
● Red #01 French Knot	
Color numbers given are for Uniek Needloft plastic canvas yarn.	

STARS & STRIPES JEWELRY

Designed by Kathy Wirth

Create a sparkling jewelry set including a star barrette and a star rainbow pin!

Skill Level: Beginner

Materials

Patriotic Star Barrette
- 2 (5") plastic canvas stars
- ⅛" metallic braid as listed in color key
- 17mm clear acrylic star
- Barrette
- Clear nylon monofilament
- Craft glue
- #18 tapestry needle

Rainbow Star Pin
- 5" plastic canvas star
- 4" x 4" piece clear 7-count plastic canvas
- ⅛" metallic braid as listed in color key
- 1 yard fine gold braid
- 17mm blue acrylic star
- Pin back
- Hot-glue gun
- #18 tapestry needle

Instructions

1. Cut plastic canvas according to graphs (Page 82), cutting 7 bars off one star for pin and 4 bars off remaining two stars for barrette.

2. Stitch according to graphs, stitching only one star for barrette and keeping braid smooth and flat on canvas.

3. For barrette, Whipstitch front and back pieces together with ⅛" gold braid. Glue clear acrylic star to front center. Sew barrette to back with monofilament.

4. For pin, Overcast star with ⅛" gold braid. Overcast rainbow with adjacent colors.

5. Whipstitch center of star to corner of rainbow with fine gold braid. Glue blue acrylic star to center of stitched star.

6. Glue pin back to back of star. ❖

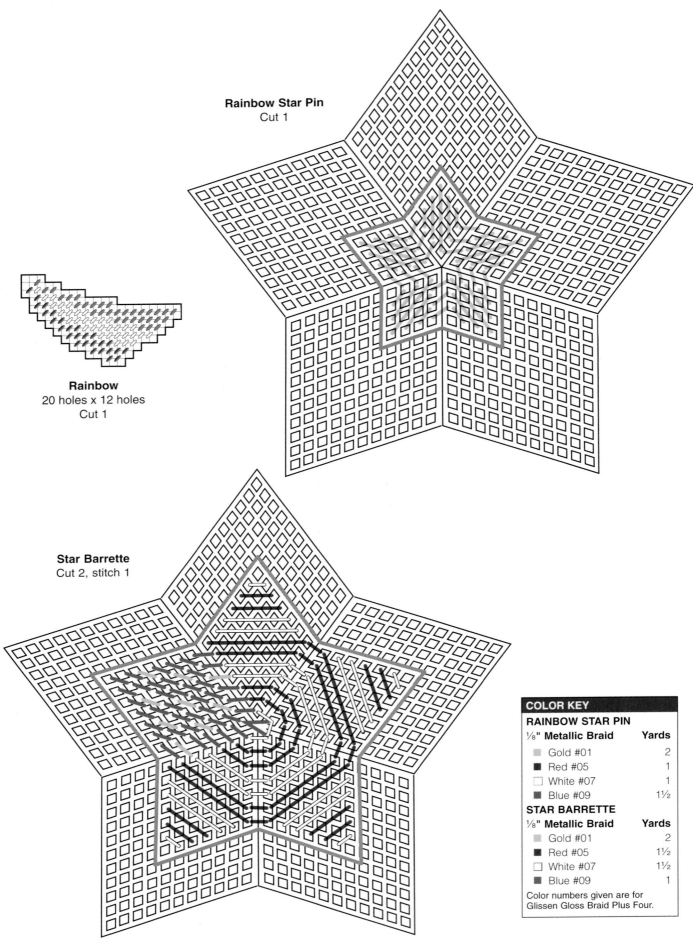

Rainbow Star Pin
Cut 1

Rainbow
20 holes x 12 holes
Cut 1

Star Barrette
Cut 2, stitch 1

COLOR KEY

RAINBOW STAR PIN

1/8" **Metallic Braid**	Yards
■ Gold #01	2
■ Red #05	1
□ White #07	1
■ Blue #09	1½

STAR BARRETTE

1/8" **Metallic Braid**	Yards
■ Gold #01	2
■ Red #05	1½
□ White #07	1½
■ Blue #09	1

Color numbers given are for
Glissen Gloss Braid Plus Four.

82

ALL-AMERICAN MUG

Designed by Karen McDanel

This mug says without a doubt that you're proud to be an American! Stitch it up in just a couple hours!

Skill Level: Beginner

Materials

- ⅓ sheet 7-count clear plastic canvas
- 4-ply worsted weight yarn as listed in color key
- White-rimmed plastic mug with insert area

Instructions

1. Cut plastic canvas piece according to graph.

2. Stitch piece according to graph, using Continental Stitches and Slanting Gobelin Stitches.

3. Overcast long edges with blue. Using white, Whipstitch short sides together to form a cylinder. Place mug insert inside mug, placing seam at mug handle.

4. Remove insert before washing mug. ❖

COLOR KEY	
4-Ply Yarn	**Yards**
■ Red	10
□ White	10
■ Midnight blue	9
▨ Gold	3

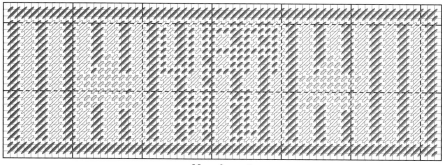

Mug Insert
63 holes x 23 holes
Cut 1

TRICKS & TREATS

Welcome autumn with a home all decked out for a spooky Halloween! Festive decorations and candy bags for trick-or-treating will bring you hours of stitching fun and squeals of delight from any little ghosts and goblins in your family.

JACK-O'-LANTERN COASTERS

Designed by Celia Lange Designs

Serve up mugs of steaming hot apple cider on these spooky jack-o'-lantern coasters! When not in use, they can be stored in the handy picket-fence holder.

Skill Level: Intermediate

Materials

- 1 sheet 10-count plastic canvas
- #5 pearl cotton as listed in color key
- #3 pearl cotton as listed in color key
- 1 sheet orange craft foam or felt
- Low-temp glue gun

Instructions

1. Cut plastic canvas according to graphs.

2. Stitch pieces following graphs, reversing one leaf before stitching.

3. Work backgrounds of jack-o'-lanterns in Continental Stitches and stem areas in Cross Stitches. Backstitch with dark mahogany over Continental Stitches. Overcast bottom third of jack-o'-lanterns between dots with medium mahogany. With bright pumpkin Overcast top ⅔ of jack-o'-lanterns. Overcast stem areas with mustard.

4. For leaves, Overcast top edges between dots with apple green and bottom edges between dots with dark willow green.

5. Overcast bottom edge of fence with dark willow green and all remaining uncharted edges with ecru. *Note: To maintain the look of the pickets, Overcast edges in same direction as long stitches.*

6. Using dark willow green throughout, Overcast top edges of box sides and front. Whipstitch back, front and box sides together and then stitch to bottom.

7. Glue wrong side of picket fence to inside back of box. Using photo as a guide, glue leaves to front of box so bottom edges of leaves and box are even.

8. Cut four circles slightly smaller than jack-o'-lanterns from craft foam sheet or felt. Glue to back of jack-o'-lanterns. ❖

COLOR KEY	
#3 Pearl Cotton	**Yards**
☐ Ecru	20½
▨ Medium mahogany #301	6
☐ Light tangerine #742	6
▨ Apricot #900	15
■ Pumpkin #971	18
■ Mustard #3045	17
■ Dark willow green #3345	18½
▨ Apple green #3347	10
Uncoded area is bright pumpkin #947 Continental Stitch	27
#5 Pearl Cotton	
╱ Dark mahogany #300 Backstitch	20
Color numbers given are for DMC #3 and #5 pearl cotton.	

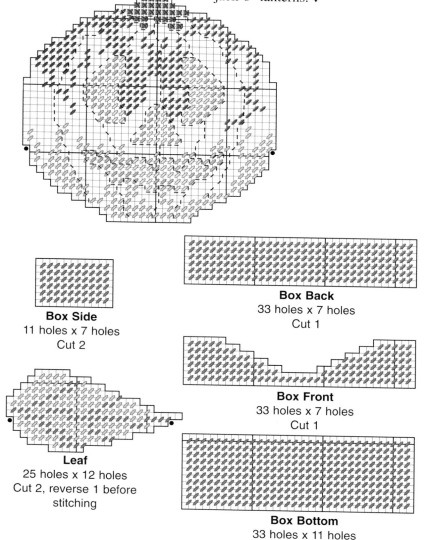

Jack-o'-Lantern
36 holes x 39 holes
Cut 4

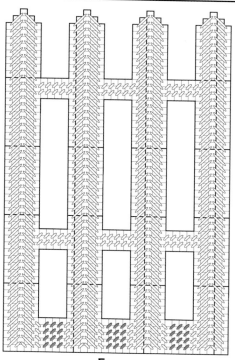

Fence
32 holes x 50 holes
Cut 1

Box Side
11 holes x 7 holes
Cut 2

Leaf
25 holes x 12 holes
Cut 2, reverse 1 before stitching

Box Back
33 holes x 7 holes
Cut 1

Box Front
33 holes x 7 holes
Cut 1

Box Bottom
33 holes x 11 holes
Cut 1

CURLY THE CLOWN

Designed by Dianne Davis

Delight your little trick-or-treater with this whimsical candy bag! Your child can fill it with treats on Halloween night, then keep it as a handy tote bag for the rest of the year!

Skill Level: Beginner

Materials

- 2 sheets clear 7-count plastic canvas
- Plastic canvas yarn as listed in color key
- #16 or #18 tapestry needle
- 4 (35mm) moving eyes
- 2 (1½") yellow pompons
- Craft glue

Instructions

1. Cut plastic canvas according to graphs. Cut one 40-hole x 20-hole piece for bag bottom. Bag bottom will remain unstitched.

2. Stitch pieces following graphs, making each Turkey Loop approximately 3" long.

3. Using white throughout, Overcast top edges of front, back and sides. Overcast long edges of handle. Whipstitch front, back and sides together and then sides to bottom.

4. Whipstitch handle to sides where indicated on graph.

5. Glue eyes and pompon noses to front and back. ❖

COLOR KEY	
Plastic Canvas Yarn	**Yards**
■ Black #00	14
▨ Lemon #20	3½
☐ White #41	66
▨ Turquoise #54	8
■ Watermelon #55	86
• Watermelon #55 Turkey loops	
• Attach nose	
= Attach handle	
Color numbers given are for Uniek Needloft plastic canvas yarn.	

Clown Bag Handle
4 holes x 90 holes
Cut 1

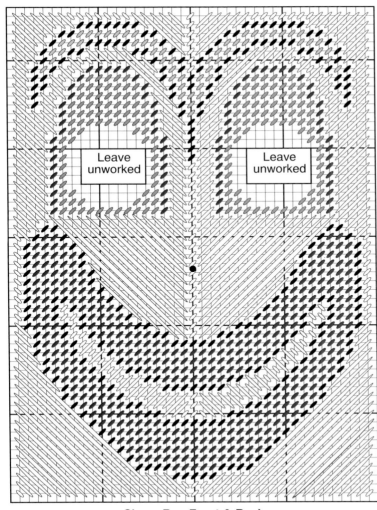

Clown Bag Front & Back
40 holes x 56 holes
Cut 2

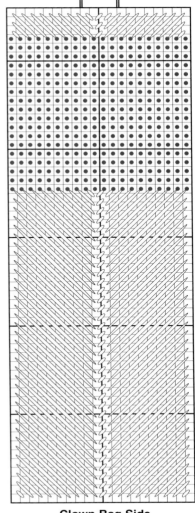

Clown Bag Side
20 holes x 56 holes
Cut 2

BLACK CAT WREATH

Designed by Jocelyn Sass

Hang this Halloween wreath on your door to welcome trick-or-treaters into your home.

Skill Level: Beginner

Materials

- 1 sheet clear 7-count plastic canvas
- Plastic canvas yarn as listed in color key
- 6-strand embroidery floss: small amounts lime green and yellow
- #16 tapestry needle
- 12" straw wreath
- ¾" bendable ribbon:
  2¼ yards orange
  1⅓ yards black
- ¼" bendable ribbon:
  1⅔ yards orange
  ⅔ yard black
- 2 (½") moon-shaped gold spangles
- Tacky craft glue
- Straight pins
- Pencil

Instructions

1. Cut plastic canvas according to graph.

2. Continental Stitch piece following graph, Overcasting in adjacent colors.

3. Cut two pieces yellow floss, 4" each. Thread under stitches indicated for whisker placement on cat's face. Trim to desired length. Glue moons to cat's face for eyes where indicated on graph.

4. Wrap ¾" orange ribbon around wreath, spacing evenly. Glue ends in back and pin in place until dry.

5. Form ¾" black ribbon into a six-loop bow. Cut narrow black ribbon in half. Wrap one end of one piece of ribbon around center of bow and twist in back to secure. Allow remaining 9" to hang down. Repeat with second piece of ribbon.

6. From narrow orange ribbon, cut one 30" piece and two 12" pieces. Form 30" piece into a six-loop bow. *Note: This will be smaller than the black bow.* Wrap each 12" piece of ribbon around bow as for black bow, allowing ends to hang down.

7. Wrap hanging ends around pencil to form spirals.

8. Glue black bow to top center of wreath. Pin in place until dry. Glue center of orange bow over center of black bow. Pin in place until dry. Glue or pin cat to lower half of wreath. ❖

COLOR KEY	
Plastic Canvas Yarn	**Yards**
■ Black #00	21
■ Fern #23	1½
■ Bright orange #58	9
6-Strand Embroidery Floss	
╱ Lime green Backstitch	
— Whisker placement	
⌒ Eye placement	
Color numbers given are for Uniek Needloft plastic canvas yarn.	

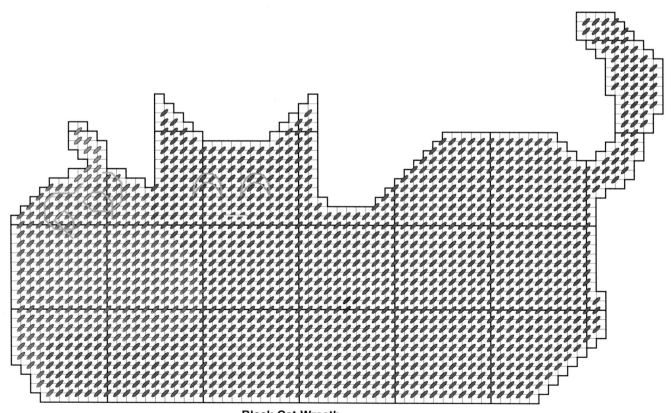

Black Cat Wreath
68 holes x 42 holes
Cut 2, reverse 1

GLOW TOTES

Designed by Rosemarie Walter

Skill Level: Beginner

Materials

- 4 sheets black 10-count plastic canvas
- ⅛" glow-in-the-dark ribbon as listed in color key
- Medium (#16) braid as listed in color key
- 20 yards black plastic canvas yarn
- Tapestry needle

Instructions

1. Cut pieces according to graphs (also see Pages 94 and 95). For each bag, cut two 105-hole x 29-hole sides and one 70-hole x 29-hole bottom.

2. For ghost tote, Satin Stitch ghost on tote front and back following graph. Backstitch and Straight Stitch chains in ghost's hands with medium braid. Backstitch chain borders and handles with lime ⅛" ribbon.

3. With black yarn, Whipstitch sides of ghost tote together then Whipstitch bottom to sides. With black yarn, Whipstitch handles to tote where indicated on graph.

4. For pumpkin tote, Satin Stitch pumpkin following graph. Backstitch borders and handles according to graph.

5. With black yarn, Whipstitch sides of pumpkin tote together then Whipstitch bottom to sides. With black yarn, Whipstitch handles to tote where indicated on graph. ❖

COLOR KEY	
⅛" Ribbon	**Yards**
■ Tangerine #051F	16
■ Grapefruit #052F	12½
■ Lime #053F	15½
▫ Lemon lime #054F	12
■ Watermelon #055F	2
Medium (#16) Braid	
■ Lime #053F	2
Color numbers given are for Kreinik ⅛" ribbon and Medium (#16) Braid.	

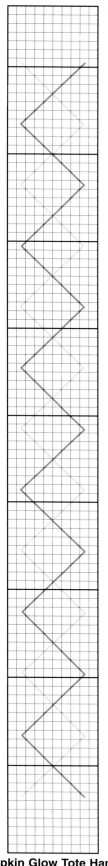

Pumpkin Glow Tote Handle
10 holes x 97 holes
Cut 2

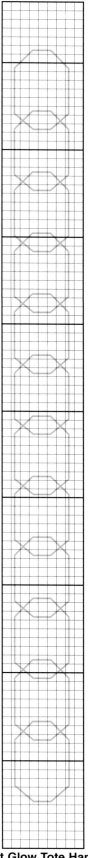

Ghost Glow Tote Handle
9 holes x 97 holes
Cut 2

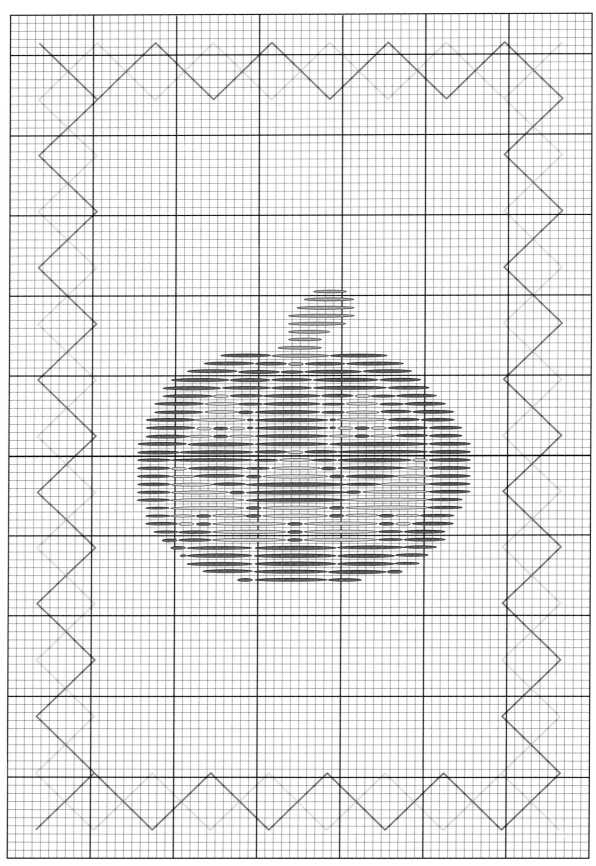

Pumpkin Glow Tote Front & Back
70 holes x 105 holes
Cut 2

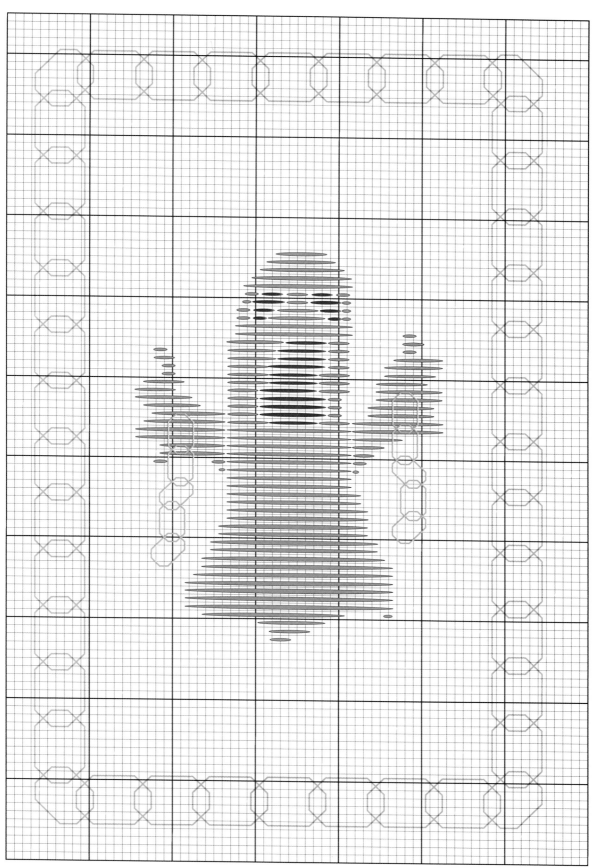

Ghost Glow Tote Front & Back
70 holes x 105 holes
Cut 2

BAT CANDY KEEPER

Designed by Kathy Wirth

Turn out the lights and watch this candy dish eerily glow! Filled with sweet treats, this fun project will delight kids and adults alike on Halloween night!

Skill Level: Intermediate

Materials

- 1 sheet 14-count black plastic canvas
- 4¼" plastic canvas circle
- 6-strand embroidery floss as listed in color key
- Fine (#8) glow-in-the-dark braid as listed in color key
- #24 tapestry needle
- 3½" x 5" piece self-adhesive black felt

Instructions

1. Cut front from black plastic canvas following graph. Cut 4½" circle in half along straightest bar for box bottom. Cut a 6" x 8" piece black plastic canvas for bat and one 59-hole x 33-hole piece from black for box back. Back will remain unstitched.

2. Stitch pieces following graphs, centering bat design before stitching. When stitching with embroidery floss, use 3 strands for Cross Stitching and 2 strands for Backstitching.

3. Carefully cut out bat at least one hole beyond stitched outline. Cut tab along cutting lines.

4. Using half-circle as a template, cut felt slightly smaller than half-circle; set aside.

5. Using 6 strands separated black floss, Overcast front to back at sides, then Whipstitch front and back to bottom with two stitches per hole on bottom piece.

6. Align point of bat's tail to center of box back. Attach tab to back with black floss, anchoring at top and bottom.

7. Peel off backing and place felt in

COLOR KEY

Fine (#8) Braid
- ■ Tangerine #051F
- ▨ Lemon-lime #054F
- ╱ Lemon-lime #054F Backstitch

6-Strand Embroidery Floss
- ■ Medium lavender #110
- ■ Black #403
- ╱ Medium lavender #110 Backstitch
- ╱ Black #403 Backstitch
- ╱ Cutting line

Color numbers given are for Kreinik Fine (#8) Glow-in-the-Dark Braid and Anchor 6-strand embroidery floss by Coats & Clark.

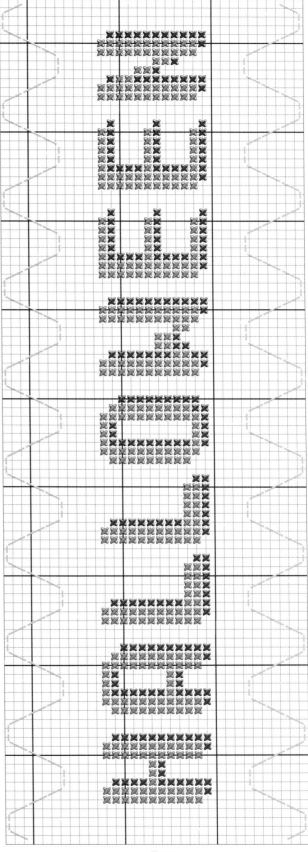

Front
95 holes x 33 holes
Cut 1

Bat
53 holes x 89 holes
Cut 1 after stitching

Designed by Mary T. Cosgrove

Skill Level: Beginner

Materials

- 1 sheet 7-count plastic canvas
- 3" plastic canvas circle
- Plastic canvas yarn: 7 yards yellow #57 and as listed in color key

Instructions

1. Cut plastic canvas according to graphs.

2. Stitch lid pieces following graphs. Overcast eye, nose and mouth edges with yellow. Overlap pumpkin faces as indicated on graph before Continental Stitching with bright orange.

3. Using bright orange throughout, Whipstitch top and bottom darts of pumpkin faces together

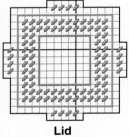

Lid
17 holes x 17 holes
Cut 1

Lid Lips
13 holes x 2 holes
Cut 4

Stem
7 holes x 9 holes
Cut 4

COLOR KEY	
Plastic Canvas Yarn	**Yards**
■ Fern #23	4
■ Bright orange #58	20
– Attach stem	
– Attach lid lips	
Color numbers given are for Uniek Needleloft plastic canvas yarn.	

Fill this smiling jack-'o-lantern with fresh potpourri to freshen up your haunted house!

at dots. Overcast top edges and Whipstitch unstitched 3" circle to bottom edges.

4. With bright orange, Overcast lid edges and bottom edges of lid lips. With fern, Whipstitch stem pieces together then Whipstitch stem to lid where indicated on graph. With bright orange, Whipstitch lid lips to lid where indicated on graph. *Note: Whipstitch lips to lid in same direction as Continental Stitches.*

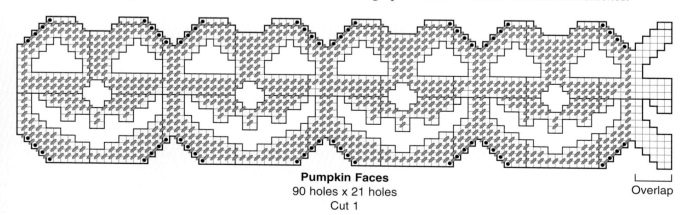

Pumpkin Faces
90 holes x 21 holes
Cut 1

Overlap

A DAY
OF THANKS

Celebrate Thanksgiving Day by reflecting on the bounty and freedom given to us by our God, and by stitching colorful Thanksgiving decorations to adorn your dinner table and home!

AUTUMN HAR

Designed by Celia Lange Designs

BARN
DANCE
7PM

AUTUMN HARVEST

WELCOME

Celebrate the beauty and bounty of our homeland during the autumn season with this friendly welcome sign!

Skill Level: Intermediate

Materials

- 2 sheets stiff 7-count plastic canvas
- Scraps 10-count plastic canvas
- Plastic canvas yarn as listed in color key
- #3 pearl cotton as listed in color key
- #5 pearl cotton as listed in color key
- 6-strand embroidery floss as listed in color key
- Toothpick
- Small bunch raffia
- Tan pipe cleaner
- 2 (1¼") lengths gold-tone medium-weight chain
- Sheet tan craft foam
- Low-temp glue gun

Instructions

1. Cut plastic canvas according to graphs (also see Page 107).

2. Stitch all pieces following graphs. Cross Stitch Pumpkin 1 with pumpkin #5 pearl cotton and Pumpkin 2 with golden brown #5 pearl cotton. Continental Stitch Pumpkin 3 with bright pumpkin #3 pearl cotton and Pumpkin 4 with apricot #3 pearl cotton.

3. Overcast welcome sign with walnut and upper edge of barn roof with coffee. Overcast all remaining edges with adjacent colors.

4. Backstitch lettering on barn dance sign with 3 strands black floss. Backstitch lettering on barn and on welcome sign with black #3 pearl cotton.

5. Using barn and welcome sign as templates, cut tan craft foam to fit, leaving small area at top of barn backing for sawtooth hanger. Stitch chains to back of barn and sign where indicated on graph. *Note: If necessary, equalize chains so sign hangs straight.* Glue craft foam in place. Glue sawtooth hanger to back of barn at top. Glue roof to top edge of barn.

6. Using photo as a guide, glue toothpick to small sign and then sign to barn. Cut eight ½" lengths of pipe cleaner and glue to backs of pumpkins for stems; glue pumpkins to barn (refer to photo for placement).

7. Cut raffia into 3¼" lengths. Set aside a small amount for loose straw (see photo). For haystack, wrap one piece of raffia around a small raffia bundle 1¼" from top; glue to secure. Glue loose straw and haystack in doorway. ❖

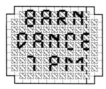

Barn Dance Sign
12 holes x 10 holes
Cut 1 from 10-count

Pumpkin 1
6 holes x 9 holes
Cut 2 from 10-count

Pumpkin 2
6 holes x 6 holes
Cut 2 from 10-count

Pumpkin 3
9 holes x 9 holes
Cut 2 from 10-count

Pumpkin 4
7 holes x 7 holes
Cut 2 from 10-count

HARVEST WEI

Designed by Darla Fanton

welce

Greet guests to your home with this colorful welcoming sign decked with a bushel of tasty autumn fruits and vegetables!

COME

Skill Level: Intermediate

Materials
- 1 artist-size sheet stiff 7-count plastic canvas
- Worsted weight yarn as listed in color key
- Straw satin raffia
- Sawtooth hanger

Instructions

1. Cut plastic canvas according to graph.

2. Stitch piece following graph. Overcast pumpkin with carrot, welcome banner with walnut and all other edges with adjacent colors.

3. Sew sawtooth hanger to center top of wrong side. ❖

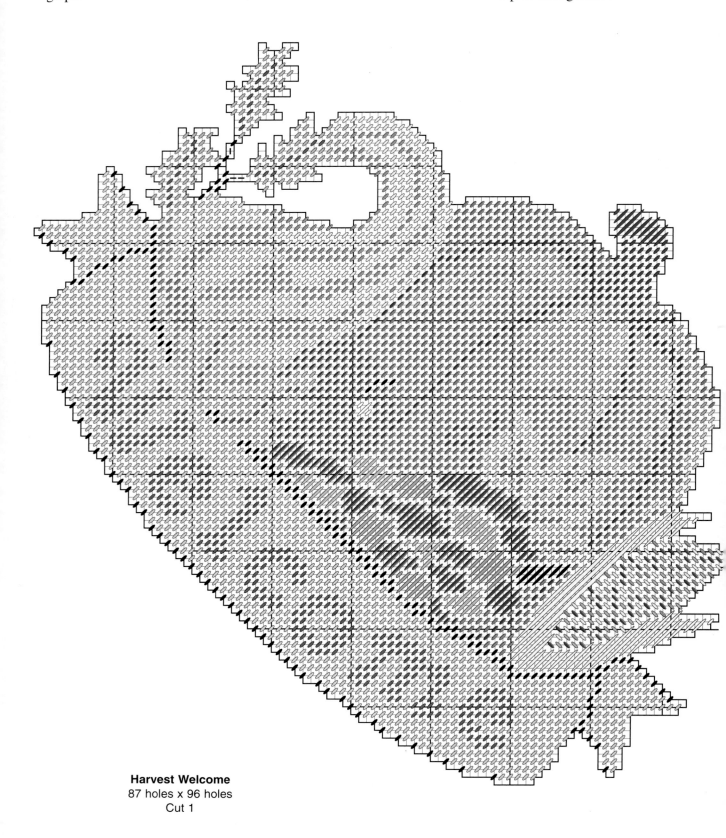

Harvest Welcome
87 holes x 96 holes
Cut 1

Continued from Page 103

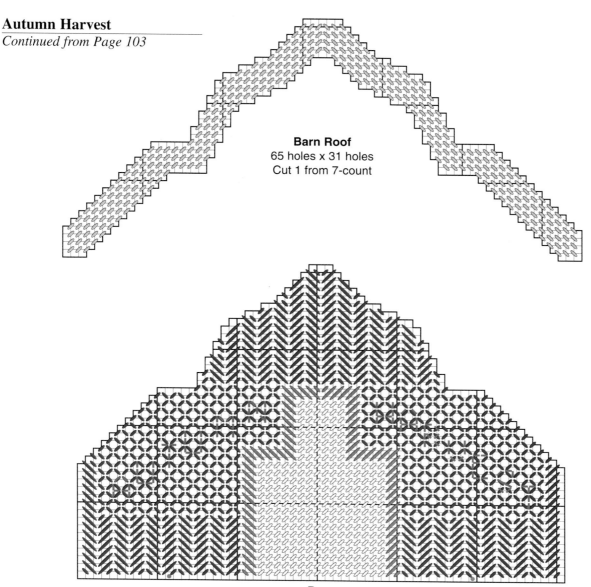

Barn Roof
65 holes x 31 holes
Cut 1 from 7-count

Barn
61 holes x 41 holes
Cut 1 from 7-count

COLOR KEY	
Plastic Canvas Yarn	**Yards**
Natural #0002	3
Wine #0011	35
Walnut #0047	10
Almond #0056	22
Coffee #0031	1
#3 Pearl Cotton	
Bright pumpkin #947	3
Apricot #900	2
/ Black #310 Backstitch	7
#5 Pearl Cotton	
Ecru	4
Pumpkin #740	3
Golden brown #977	2
6-Strand Embroidery Floss	
/ Black #310 Backstitch	
• Attach chain	

Color numbers given are for Spinrite plastic canvas yarn and DMC #3 and #5 pearl cotton and 6-strand embroidery floss.

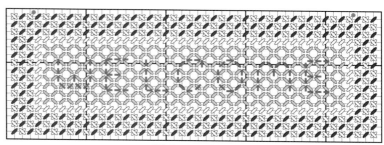

Welcome Sign
47 holes x 17 holes
Cut 1 from 7-count

CORNUCOPIA PLACE MAT

Designed by Michele Wilcox

Set your Thanksgiving dinner table with festive place mats displaying a cornucopia generously filled with fruit of the land!

Skill Level: Beginner

Materials

- 90-hole x 70-hole sheet 7-count plastic canvas
- Plastic canvas yarn as listed in color key

Instructions

1. Continental Stitch piece following graph.
2. Overcast edges with holly. ❖

Cornucopia Place Mat
90 holes x 70 holes
Cut 1

COLOR KEY	
Plastic Canvas Yarn	**Yards**
■ Red #01	4
■ Cinnamon #14	4
▨ Gold #17	12
▨ Mint #24	4
■ Holly #27	34
▨ Gray #38	4
☐ Eggshell #39	26
■ Purple #46	4
☐ Yellow #57	3
▨ Bright orange #58	2
▨ Plum #59	3
Color numbers given are for Uniek Needloft plastic canvas yarn.	

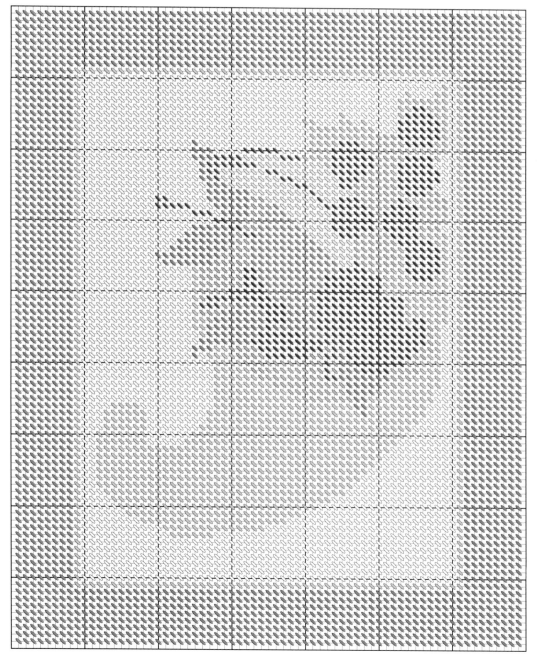

109

LITTLE PILGRIM

Designed by Michele Wilcox

While Miss Pilgrim proudly holds her garden's first pumpkin in her arms, prop a door open with this adorable little doorstop and let the cool, crisp autumn breezes inside!

Skill Level: Beginner

Materials

- 1½ sheets 7-count plastic canvas
- Plastic canvas yarn as listed in color key
- #3 pearl cotton as listed in color key
- Hot-glue gun

Instructions

1. Cut plastic canvas according to graphs.

2. Stitch pieces following graphs, reversing one arm before stitching. Use 6 strands floss for embroidery. Overcast Pilgrim head with white, shoes with black and body with silver; Overcast arms and pumpkin with adjacent colors.

3. With mint, Overcast bottom edges of doorstop sides; Whipstitch sides together and then sides to top.

4. Glue Pilgrim to one large side so that bottom edges of side and feet are even. Using photo as a guide, glue pumpkin at an angle to front of Pilgrim. Glue arms in place at shoulders and sides so one hand is on top of the other in front of pumpkin. ❖

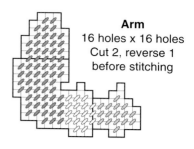

Arm
16 holes x 16 holes
Cut 2, reverse 1
before stitching

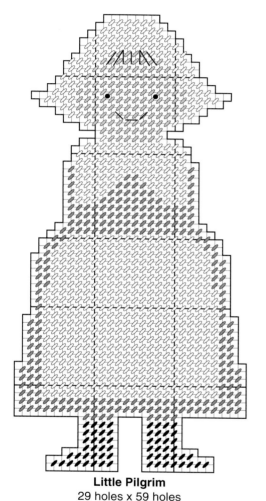

Little Pilgrim
29 holes x 59 holes
Cut 1

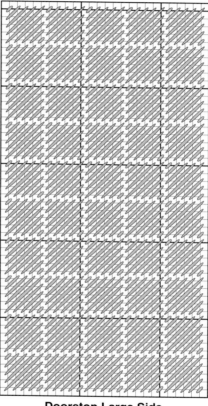

Doorstop Large Side
26 holes x 51 holes
Cut 2

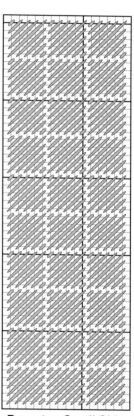

Doorstop Small Side
16 holes x 51 holes
Cut 2

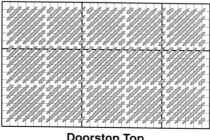

Doorstop Top
26 holes x 16 holes
Cut 1

Pumpkin
17 holes x 15 holes
Cut 1

COLOR KEY	
Plastic Canvas Yarn	**Yards**
■ Black #00	2
▨ Pumpkin #12	4
▨ Mint #24	60
▨ Silver #37	12
☐ White #41	16
▨ Fleshtone #56	3
#3 Pearl Cotton	
• Black French Knot	1
╱ Black Straight Stitch	
Color numbers given are for Uniek Needloft plastic canvas yarn.	

Thanksgiving Place Card Holders

Designed by Michele Wilcox

Theresa

Michael

Ashley

Jonathan

Seat your Thanksgiving dinner guests with these adorable projects! Each is quick and easy to stitch and sure to delight all.

Skill Level: Beginner

Materials
- 1¼ sheets 7-count plastic canvas
- Plastic canvas yarn as listed in color key
- Hot-glue gun
- 4 (2¾" x 3") pieces poster board

Instructions
1. Cut plastic canvas according to graphs.

2. Continental Stitch pieces following graphs. Overcast inside edges of place card holder fronts and bottom edges of both fronts and backs with cerulean. With wrong sides together, Whipstitch place card holder fronts and backs together along side and top edges with cerulean.

3. Overcast edges of remaining pieces with adjacent colors.

Overcast turkey beak and leg with yellow.

4. Where indicated on graph, glue stand to back of place card holder along top edges. Using photo as a guide, glue turkey, hat, pumpkin and corn to upper right front edge of place card holders.

5. Write names on center of poster board pieces and insert into place card holders. ❖

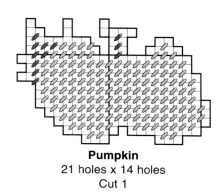

Pumpkin
21 holes x 14 holes
Cut 1

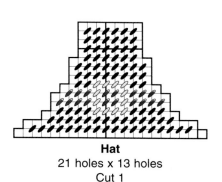

Hat
21 holes x 13 holes
Cut 1

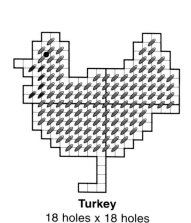

Turkey
18 holes x 18 holes
Cut 1

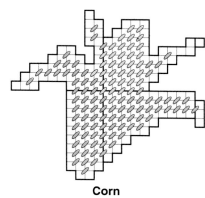

Corn
21 holes x 19 holes
Cut 1

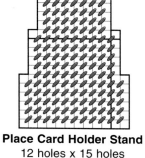

Place Card Holder Stand
12 holes x 15 holes
Cut 4

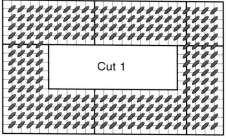

Place Card Holder Front
24 holes x 15 holes
Cut 4

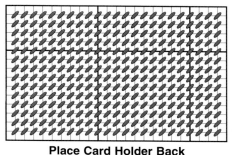

Place Card Holder Back
24 holes x 15 holes
Cut 4

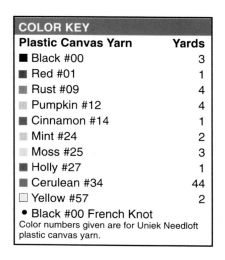

COLOR KEY	
Plastic Canvas Yarn	**Yards**
■ Black #00	3
■ Red #01	1
■ Rust #09	4
▨ Pumpkin #12	4
■ Cinnamon #14	1
▨ Mint #24	2
▨ Moss #25	3
■ Holly #27	1
■ Cerulean #34	44
☐ Yellow #57	2
• Black #00 French Knot	

Color numbers given are for Uniek Needloft plastic canvas yarn.

TEDDY BEAR'S THANKSGIVING

Designed by Michele Wilcox

Tuck a boutique box of tissues inside this delightful little bear Pilgrim! He's a charming decorative accent that's practical too!

Skill Level: Beginner

Materials

- 1¼ sheets 7-count plastic canvas
- Plastic canvas yarn as listed in color key
- #3 pearl cotton as listed in color key

Instructions

1. Cut plastic canvas according to graphs.

2. Continental Stitch pieces following the graphs. With avocado green #3 pearl cotton, Backstitch pumpkins. With black #3 pearl cotton, Backstitch mouths and outlines around teddy bears; work French Knots for eyes.

3. With eggshell, Overcast bottom edges of sides and inner edges of top. With eggshell, Whipstitch sides together and then top to sides. ❖

COLOR KEY	
Plastic Canvas Yarn	**Yards**
■ Black #00	5
▨ Mint #24	5
☐ Eggshell #39	40
■ Crimson #42	2
▨ Camel #43	36
▨ Bittersweet #52	10
▨ Yellow #57	1
#3 Pearl Cotton	
● Black #310 French Knot	16½
╱ Black #310 Backstitch	
╱ Avocado green #580 Backstitch	6
Color numbers given are for Uniek Needloft plastic canvas yarn and DMC #3 pearl cotton.	

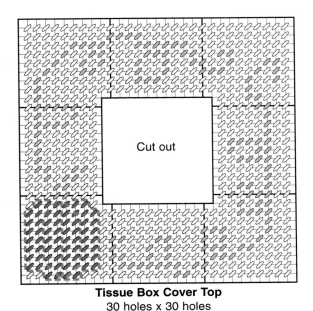

Tissue Box Cover Top
30 holes x 30 holes
Cut 1

Tissue Box Cover Side
30 holes x 36 holes
Cut 4

Christmas Celebrations

Celebrate the Christmas season with peace, goodwill and cheer to all by making and sharing festive decorations and gifts! Delight your loved ones with a Christmas tree decked with beautiful hand-stitched ornaments, with pretty and practical gift boxes, with jewelry nestled in the bottom of their stocking, and so much more—all beautifully worked with plastic canvas!

CHRISTMAS CRITTERS

Designed by Vicki Blizzard

Delight your children or grandchildren with a set of these whimsical Christmas ornaments! A puppy, kitten, bunny, flamingo and mice will trim your tree with holiday happiness!

Skill Level: Intermediate

Materials

All Ornaments
- Plastic canvas yarn as listed in color key
- 15" fine gold (#8) metallic braid
- #16 tapestry needle
- Polyester fiberfill
- Hot-glue gun

Flamingo
- ½ sheet 7-count plastic canvas
- 2 (3mm) black round cabochons
- 8 (3mm) ruby round cabochons
- 6" ⅛"-wide red satin ribbon
- ¼" white pompon

Mice in a Stocking
- ½ sheet 7-count plastic canvas
- 4 (6mm) black round cabochons
- 18" ⅛"-wide green satin ribbon

Kitten in a Mitten
- ½ sheet 7-count plastic canvas
- 2 (8mm) black round cabochons
- 6" ⅛"-wide green satin ribbon

Bunny in a Hat
- ½ sheet 7-count plastic canvas
- 2 (8mm) black round cabochons
- 3 (3mm) ruby round cabochons
- 12" ⅛"-wide green satin ribbon
- 1"-wide piece of cardboard

Puppy in a Wreath
- 1 sheet 7-count plastic canvas
- 2 (8mm) black round cabochons
- 12 (3mm) ruby round cabochons
- 1 yard ⅛"-wide red satin ribbon

Flamingo

1. Cut plastic canvas according to graphs (Page 120).

2. Stitch pieces following graphs, reversing one body and one wing before stitching. Stitch four leaves with clover and four with brisk green.

3. Whipstitch wrong sides of body together with adjacent colors, stuffing body only, not neck and head, with fiberfill before closing. Overcast wings, leaves and wreath with adjacent colors.

4. Overcast all side and bottom edges of hat dangle with scarlet. Overcast bottom edges of hat pieces with white. With wrong sides together, Whipstitch side edges of hat together with adjacent colors. Whipstitch top edges of hat and hat

dangle together with scarlet.

5. Using photo as a guide, glue wing to each side of body. For tail feathers, cut four 6" lengths of cherry blossom. Thread one length through each hole where indicated on graph with blue dots; tie yarn in a knot and trim all pieces evenly.

6. Using photo as a guide, glue one black cabochon to each side of head for eyes, one foot perpendicular to bottom of each leg and legs to bottom of body.

7. Using photo as a guide, glue leaves to wrong side of wreath base, alternating colors and overlapping slightly. Glue ruby cabochons to leaves where indicated on graph. Tie red ribbon in a bow and glue to bottom of wreath. Slide wreath over flamingo's head and down neck to body.

8. Glue pompon to point on hat dangle. Place hat as desired on head and glue in place.

9. Thread gold braid through top of body; tie ends in a knot to form a loop for hanging.

Mice in a Stocking

1. Cut pieces according to graphs (Page 121).

2. Stitch pieces following graphs, reversing one stocking piece before stitching. Stitch four ears with cherry blossom and four with silver gray.

3. Whipstitch wrong sides of two head pieces together with silver gray, stuffing firmly with fiberfill before closing. Repeat with remaining head pieces. For ears, Whipstitch wrong side of one cherry blossom piece and wrong side of one silver gray piece together with silver gray. Repeat with remaining ear pieces.

4. Overcast area indicated on each muzzle with cherry blossom. Overcast remaining muzzle edges and paw edges with silver gray. Using 2 plies cherry blossom, add Straight Stitches to muzzles and paws and French Knots to muzzles.

5. Using scarlet throughout, Overcast top edges of stockings, then

Whipstitch wrong sides of stockings together.

6. Using photo as a guide, glue one muzzle to each head, then black cabochons to faces. Glue ears to sides of heads with cherry blossom sides facing front.

7. Cut green ribbon in half and tie each length in a bow around necks, trimming ends evenly. Stuff stocking with fiberfill to bottom edge of top band. Using photo as a guide, glue mice inside top of stocking, overlapping slightly. Glue paws to front top edge of stocking.

8. For tails, cut two 5" lengths of silver gray. Glue one length behind each mouse toward outside edges. Trim tails to desired length; tie ends in knots to prevent fraying.

9. Thread gold braid through center back edge at top of stocking; tie ends in a knot to form a loop for hanging.

Kitten in a Mitten

1. Cut pieces according to graphs (Page 122).

2. Stitch pieces following graphs, reversing one mitten before stitching. Stitch one ear with cherry blossom as shown; reverse one and stitch with cherry blossom. Stitch one ear with white; reverse last piece and stitch with white.

3. Whipstitch wrong sides of two head pieces together with white, stuffing firmly with fiberfill before closing. For ears, Whipstitch wrong side of one cherry blossom piece and wrong side of one white piece together with cherry blossom where indicated on graph; Whipstitch remaining edges with white. Repeat with remaining ear pieces.

4. Overcast area indicated on muzzle with cherry blossom. Overcast remaining muzzle edges and paw and nose edges with adjacent colors. Using 2 plies cherry blossom, add Straight Stitches to muzzle and paws and French Knots to muzzle.

5. Using brisk green throughout, Overcast top edges of mittens, then Whipstitch wrong sides of mittens together. Stuff mitten with fiberfill to top of thumb.

6. Using photo as a guide, glue nose to center top front of muzzle, muzzle to head, then black cabochons to face on each side of nose. Glue ears to sides of head with cherry blossom sides facing front.

7. Tie green ribbon in a bow and glue under one ear. Trim ends evenly. Using photo as a guide, glue head to inside top of mitten and paws to front top edge of mitten.

8. Thread gold braid through top center of head; tie ends in a knot to form a loop for hanging.

Bunny in a Hat

1. Cut pieces according to graphs (Page 122).

2. Stitch pieces following graphs. Stitch one straight ear and one folded ear bottom with cherry blossom as shown, reverse remaining pieces, and stitch with sand.

3. Whipstitch wrong sides of head pieces together with sand, stuffing head with fiberfill before closing.

4. Whipstitch wrong sides of straight ear pieces and wrong sides of folded ear bottom pieces together with sand, leaving top edges of folded ear bottom unstitched. Overcast side and bottom edges of folded ear top with sand, then Whipstitch top edge of folded ear top to top edges of folded ear bottom.

5. Using white throughout, Overcast top edges of hat, then Whipstitch wrong sides of hat together

along remaining sides. Overcast area indicated on muzzle with cherry blossom and remaining edges with white. Overcast all remaining pieces with adjacent colors. Using 2 plies cherry blossom, add Straight Stitches to muzzle and paws.

6. Using photo as a guide, glue nose to center front of muzzle, muzzle to face and one ear to each side of head. Glue ruby cabochons to bottom center of leaf, then glue leaf to head under straight ear.

7. Tie ribbon in a bow around neck; trim ends evenly. Stuff hat with fiberfill to middle of top band. Using photo as a guide, glue head to inside top of hat, paws to top front edge of hat at shoulders and black cabochons to face.

Flamingo

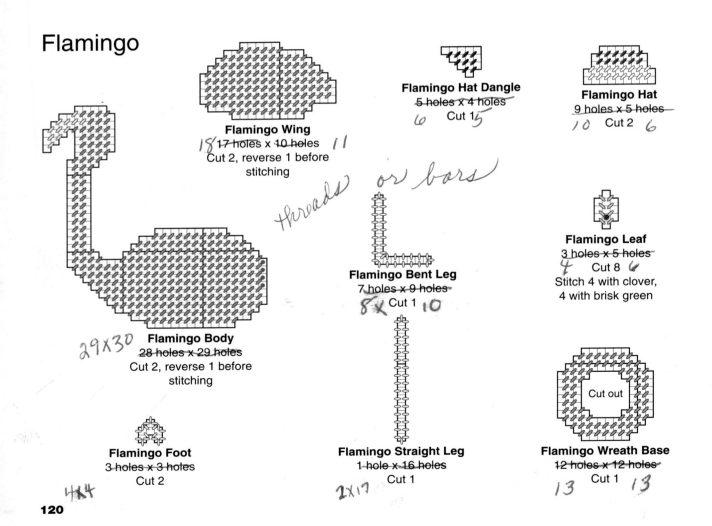

Flamingo Wing
18 17 holes x 10 holes 11
Cut 2, reverse 1 before stitching

Flamingo Hat Dangle
5 holes x 4 holes
6   Cut 1 5

Flamingo Hat
9 holes x 5 holes
10   Cut 2   6

threads or bars

Flamingo Bent Leg
7 holes x 9 holes
8 x   Cut 1   10

Flamingo Leaf
3 holes x 5 holes
4   Cut 8 6
Stitch 4 with clover,
4 with brisk green

Flamingo Body
28 holes x 29 holes
29 X 30   Cut 2, reverse 1 before stitching

Flamingo Foot
3 holes x 3 holes
Cut 2
4 x 4

Flamingo Straight Leg
1 hole x 16 holes
Cut 1
2 X 17

Flamingo Wreath Base
12 holes x 12 holes
Cut 1
13   13

Cut out

8. Cut a 3-yard length of white yarn and wrap around 1"-wide cardboard. Slide loops off cardboard and tie an 8" length of white yarn tightly around center. Cut loops and trim to form a pompon. Tie pompon to bottom center of hat.

9. Thread gold braid through center top of head; tie ends in a knot to form a loop for hanging.

Puppy in a Wreath

1. Cut plastic canvas according to graphs (Page 123), reversing one tail before stitching.

2. Stitch pieces following graphs. Stitch six leaves with clover and six with brisk green.

3. With wrong sides together, Whipstitch body pieces together with natural, stuffing head and body firm-ly with fiberfill before closing. With wrong sides together, Whipstitch tail pieces together with almond.

4. Whipstitch dart on ears together, then Overcast remaining edges of ears and area indicated on muzzle graph with almond. Overcast remaining edges of muzzle and all paw pieces with natural and all edges on remaining pieces with adjacent colors. Using 2 plies almond, add Straight Stitches to muzzle and top paws and French Knots to muzzle.

5. Using photo as a guide, glue leaves to wrong side of wreath base, alternating colors and overlapping slightly. Glue ruby cabochons to leaves where indicated on graph.

6. Cut two 12" lengths of red ribbon. Holding both lengths together, tie ribbon in a bow. Glue bow to bottom of wreath, trimming ends as desired.

7. Using photo as a guide, glue nose to center front top of muzzle and tongue to center back bottom of muzzle. Glue muzzle to face, then glue black cabochons to face. Glue one ear to each side of head.

8. Glue body to back bottom of wreath then glue top and bottom paws to body, positioning top paws slightly over inside of wreath (see photo). Glue tail to body where indicated on graph.

9. Tie remaining length of red ribbon in a bow around neck, trimming ends evenly. Thread gold braid through center top of wreath base; tie ends in a knot to form a loop for hanging. ❖

Mice in a Stocking

Mouse Paw
4 holes x 3 holes
Cut 4

Mouse Muzzle
5 holes x 4 holes
Cut 2

Mouse Ear
4 holes x 4 holes
Cut 8
Stitch 4 with cherry blossom,
4 with silver gray

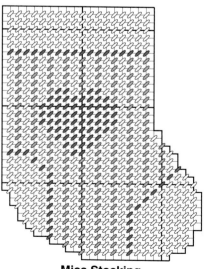

Mice Stocking
25 holes x 33 holes
Cut 2, reverse 1 before stitching

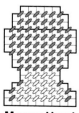

Mouse Head
9 holes x 13 holes
Cut 2

COLOR KEY	
Plastic Canvas Yarn	**Yards**
☐ White #0001	43
☐ Natural #0002	28
▨ Cherry blossom #0010	21
■ Scarlet #0022	22
▨ Brisk green #0027	37
▨ Clover #0042	8
☐ Mustard #0043	3
▨ Silver gray #0045	11
▨ Sand #0049	10
▨ Almond #0056	14
╱ Cherry blossom #0010 Straight Stitch	
● Cherry blossom #0010 French Knot	
╱ Almond #0056 Straight Stitch	
● Almond #0056 French Knot	
● Attach ruby cabochon	
╱ Attach puppy tail	
Color numbers given are for Darice Nylon Plus plastic canvas yarn.	

Kitten in a Mitten

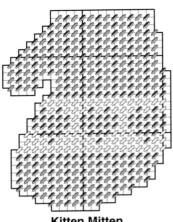

Kitten Mitten
21 holes x 26 holes
Cut 2, reverse 1 before stitching

Kitten Paw
6 holes x 4 holes
Cut 2

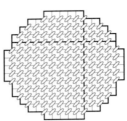

Kitten Head
15 holes x 14 holes
Cut 2

Kitten Nose
3 holes x 3 holes
Cut 1

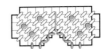

Kitten Muzzle
11 holes x 5 holes
Cut 1

Kitten Ear
4 holes x 5 holes
Cut 4, reverse 2 before stitching
Stitch 2 with cherry blossom,
2 with white

Bunny in a Hat

Bunny Nose
4 holes x 3 holes
Cut 1

Bunny Holly Leaf
5 holes x 7 holes
Cut 1

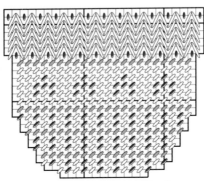

Bunny Hat Front & Back
25 holes x 22 holes
Cut 2

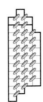

Bunny Straight Ear
4 holes x 12 holes
Cut 2, reverse 1 before stitching
Stitch 1 as shown with cherry blossom
Stitch reversed ear with sand

Bunny Paw
6 holes x 4 holes
Cut 2

Bunny Muzzle
11 holes x 5 holes
Cut 1

Bunny Folded Ear Top
4 holes x 5 holes
Cut 1

Bunny Folded Ear Bottom
4 holes x 8 holes
Cut 2, reverse 1 before stitching
Stitch 1 as shown with cherry blossom
Stitch reversed ear with sand

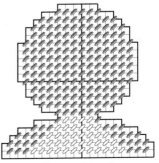

Bunny Head
19 holes x 20 holes
Cut 2

Puppy in a Wreath

Puppy Bottom Paw
5 holes x 6 holes
Cut 2

Puppy Top Paw
6 holes x 5 holes
Cut 2

Puppy Ear
5 holes x 8 holes
Cut 2

Puppy Muzzle
11 holes x 5 holes
Cut 1

Puppy Nose
5 holes x 3 holes
Cut 1

Puppy Tongue
4 holes x 4 holes
Cut 1

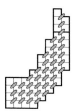

Puppy Tail
8 holes x 13 holes
Cut 2, reverse 1 before stitching

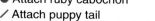

COLOR KEY	
Plastic Canvas Yarn	**Yards**
☐ White #0001	43
☐ Natural #0002	28
☐ Cherry blossom #0010	21
■ Scarlet #0022	22
■ Brisk green #0027	37
☐ Clover #0042	8
☐ Mustard #0043	3
■ Silver gray #0045	11
■ Sand #0049	10
☐ Almond #0056	14
╱ Cherry blossom #0010 Straight Stitch	
● Cherry blossom #0010 French Knot	
╱ Almond #0056 Straight Stitch	
● Almond #0056 French Knot	
● Attach ruby cabochon	
╱ Attach puppy tail	

Color numbers given are for Darice Nylon Plus plastic canvas yarn.

Puppy Leaf
7 holes x 10 holes
Cut 12
Stitch 6 with brisk green,
6 with clover

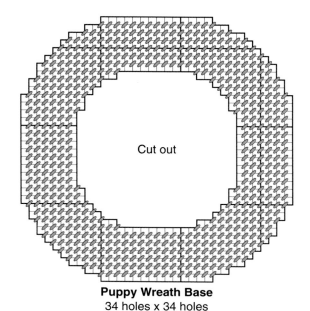

Cut out

Puppy Wreath Base
34 holes x 34 holes
Cut 1

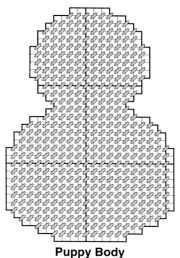

Puppy Body
21 holes x 30 holes
Cut 2

Designed by Celia Lange Designs

Skill Level: Intermediate

Poinsettia Pin & Barrette

Materials

- Small amount 14-count plastic canvas
- 6-strand embroidery floss as listed in color key
- Metallic braid as listed in color key
- ¾" pin back
- 3" barrette
- Hot-glue gun

Instructions

1. Cut plastic canvas according to graphs (Page 126).

2. Use 4 strands floss for Cross Stitching. For poinsettia fronts, stitch two pieces following graph. Reverse remaining two pieces and Cross Stitch entirely with Christmas red. For fronts only, work French Knots with gold braid and Straight Stitches with 1 strand black floss.

3. Cross Stitch barrette following graph, eliminating gold Straight Stitches for back.

4. Whipstitch wrong sides of barrettes together with gold braid. With wrong sides together and matching petals, Whipstitch poinsettia fronts and backs together with gold braid.

5. Glue one poinsettia to top of barrette piece, then glue 3" barrette to back of stitched barrette piece. Glue pin to back of remaining poinsettia.

Candy Cane Pin

Materials

- Small amount 14-count plastic canvas
- 6-strand embroidery floss as listed in color key
- ¾" pin back
- 6mm jingle bell
- 1" square gold metallic knit fabric

JEWELRY

Wear a little sparkle of Christmas all throughout the holiday season! These pieces of jewelry make great stocking stuffers too!

• Hot-glue gun

Instructions

1. Cut plastic canvas according to graph (Page 126).

2. Use 4 strands floss for Cross Stitching. Stitch one candy cane following graph for candy cane front. Reverse remaining candy cane and Cross Stitch entirely with white.

3. Whipstitch wrong sides together with adjacent colors, matching red, green and white stripes on candy cane front.

4. Gather gold fabric in center to form a bow and glue to candy cane front where indicated on graph. Glue jingle bell to center gathers of fabric; glue pin to back of candy cane.

Sleigh Pin

Materials

• Small amount 14-count plastic canvas
• 6-strand embroidery floss as listed in color key
• Metallic braid as listed in color key
• ¾" pin back
• Hot-glue gun

Instructions

1. Cut plastic canvas according to graph (Page 126).

2. Use 4 strands floss for Cross Stitching. For sleigh front, stitch one sleigh following graph. Reverse remaining sleigh and Cross Stitch entirely with Christmas green.

3. Work Backstitches over Cross Stitches on sleigh front only, using 2 strands floss for large stars and 1 strand floss for small stars. Whipstitch wrong sides together following graph, using 2 strands red floss where indicated.

4. Glue pin back to back of sleigh. ❖

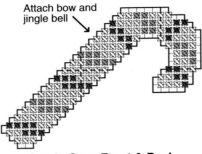

Attach bow and
jingle bell →

Candy Cane Front & Back
25 holes x 18 holes
Cut 2
Stitch 1 as graphed
Reverse 1 and Cross Stitch
entirely with white

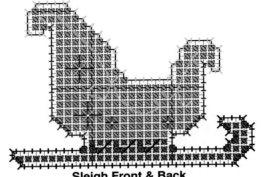

Sleigh Front & Back
30 holes x 21 holes
Cut 2
Stitch 1 as graphed
Reverse 1 and Cross Stitch
entirely with bright Christmas green

COLOR KEY	
CANDY CANE PIN	
6-Strand Embroidery Floss	**Skeins**
☐ White	1
■ Christmas red #321	1
■ Bright Christmas green #700	1
Color numbers given are for DMC 6-strand embroidery floss.	

COLOR KEY	
SLEIGH PIN	
6-Strand Embroidery Floss	**Yards**
■ Black #310	4
■ Christmas red #321	2
■ Bright Christmas green #700	8¾
╱ White Backstitch	1
╱ Christmas red #321 Backstitch and Overcasting	
╱ Bright Christmas green #700 Backstitch	
Metallic Braid	
╱ Silver #01 Backstitch and Overcasting	3
╱ Gold #03 Backstitch and Overcasting	3
Color numbers given are for DMC 6-strand embroidery floss and Madeira GlissenGloss Braid.	

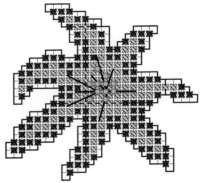

Poinsettia Front & Back
24 holes x 23 holes
Cut 4
Stitch 2 fronts as graphed
Reverse 2 and Cross Stitch
entirely with Christmas red

COLOR KEY	
POINSETTIA PIN & BARRETTE	
6-Strand Embroidery Floss	**Yards**
■ Christmas red #321	17½
■ Garnet #815	8¾
╱ Black #310 Straight Stitch	4
Metallic Braid	
● Gold #03 French Knot	3
╱ Gold #03 Long Stitch	
Color numbers given are for DMC 6-strand embroidery floss and Madeira GlissenGloss Braid.	

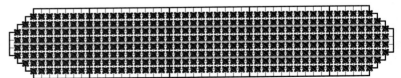

Barrette Front & Back
48 holes x 9 holes
Cut 2
Stitch front as graphed
Stitch back without
gold Straight Stitches

Ice Castle Ornament

Designed by Celia Lange Designs

Watch this ornament sparkle and dance in the light of your Christmas tree. It is stitched with glistening braid and decorated with gems.

Skill Level: Beginner

Materials

- ¼ sheet 10-count plastic canvas
- Metallic braid as listed in color key
- 10mm dark sapphire square faceted gem
- 7mm dark sapphire round faceted gem
- 2 (7mm) crystal round faceted gems
- Low-temp glue gun

Instructions

1. Cut plastic canvas according to graphs.

2. Stitch pieces following graphs, Overcasting door in blue and all other pieces in silver.

3. Glue Tower A to left side of castle, making bottom and left side edges even with castle. Glue Tower B to right side of castle, making edges even. Glue door to center front of castle. Glue gems where indicated on graphs.

4. With iridescent white, attach loop to center top of castle. ❖

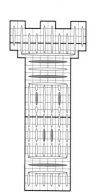

Tower A
10 holes x 23 holes
Cut 1

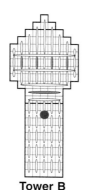

Tower B
9 holes x 29 holes
Cut 1

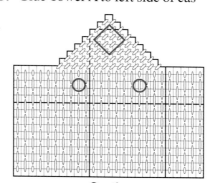

Castle
25 holes x 22 holes
Cut 1

Door
5 holes x 9 holes
Cut 1

COLOR KEY	
Metallic Braid	**Yards**
▨ Silver #03	3
☐ Iridescent white #07	8
▨ Sapphire #09	2
╱ Sapphire #09 Backstitch	
◇ Attach dark sapphire square gem	
● Attach dark sapphire round gem	
○ Attach crystal round gem	

Color numbers given are for Madeira Braid Plus Two.

HANUKKAH DREIDEL

Designed by Celia Lange Designs

Jewish children will enjoy playing a game of chance with this colorful dreidel during Hanukkah. This four-sided toy has a Hebrew letter on each side.

Skill Level: Intermediate

Materials

- 1 sheet 7-count plastic canvas
- Plastic canvas yarn as listed in color key
- 10" ¼"-diameter wooden dowel
- White acrylic paint
- Pencil sharpener
- Low-temp glue gun

Instructions

1. Cut plastic canvas according to graphs.

2. Stitch pieces following graphs. Work all Whipstitching with Cross Stitches. With robin, Whipstitch sides together in the order shown in Fig. 1 to form the box.

3. With robin, Whipstitch top edges of bottom pieces to bottom edges of sides, then Whipstitch sides of bottom pieces together. Overcast bottom edges with robin.

4. With pencil sharpener, sharpen one end of dowel to blunt point. Paint 2"–3" of pointed end with white. Allow to dry.

5. Wrap and glue a strand of yarn around dowel several times approximately 1½" from pointed end. Insert dowel into box, sliding point out opening at bottom; glue in place.

Slide top down over dowel and Whipstitch top to sides with robin.
6. With robin, Whipstitch long edges of handle sides together, then Whipstitch cap to handle. Overcast

bottom edges of handle with robin. Slide handle over dowel, trimming dowel as necessary to fit. Glue handle to top of dreidel. ❖

FIG. 1

Shin	Hay	Gimel	Nun

COLOR KEY

Plastic Canvas Yarn Yards
☐ White #01		30
▨ Robin #16		30
■ Royal #26		8

Color numbers given are for Spinrite plastic canvas yarn.

Bottom
22 holes x 11 holes
Cut 4

Handle Cap
2 holes x 2 holes
Cut 1

Shin Side
22 holes x 24 holes
Cut 1

Top
22 holes x 22 holes
Cut 1

Cut out

Handle Side
2 holes x 30 holes
Cut 4

Hay Side
22 holes x 24 holes
Cut 1

Gimel Side
22 holes x 24 holes
Cut 1

Nun Side
22 holes x 24 holes
Cut 1

129

PEPPERMINT SLEIGH

Designed by Celia Lange Designs

Decorated with peppermint sticks and candies, this festive dish will take you on a delightful winter's journey through Christmas candyland!

Skill Level: Intermediate

Materials

- 2 sheets stiff 7-count plastic canvas
- 2 (3") radial circles
- Plastic canvas yarn as listed in color key
- #3 pearl cotton as listed in color key
- Sheet brown craft foam
- Sheet white craft foam
- Hot-glue gun

Instructions

1. Cut plastic canvas according to graphs (also see Page 132). Cut away outer threads on circles so only the four innermost circles are left.

2. Stitch pieces following graphs, reversing one sleigh side, one box side, one runner brace and one candy cane runner before stitching. Work embroidery over walnut Cross Stitching on sleigh sides.

3. Overcast sleigh sides, runner braces, candy cane runners, spearmint leaves and hearts with adjacent colors.

4. Long Stitch circles in alternating white and wine stripes across three innermost threads, using three white stitches then two wine stitches all around. Work Cross Stitch in center of circle. Overcast circles in alternating white and wine yarn, using two white stitches then one wine stitch all around.

5. Cut brown craft foam slightly smaller than box pieces; set aside. With brown, Overcast top edges of box sides, front and back. To form box, Whipstitch box sides to box front and back with walnut, then Whipstitch box bottom to box. Glue craft foam to inside of box.

6. Cut brown craft foam slightly smaller than sleigh sides, then glue to backs of sleigh sides. Glue sleigh sides to box sides.

7. Using photo as a guide, glue candy cane runners to bottom of runner braces, making sure bottom edges are even. Glue runner braces to sleigh sides.

8. Using photo as a guide, glue hearts, spearmint leaves and peppermints to sleigh sides and upper runner braces. Cut white craft foam to fit backs of candy cane runners beyond runner braces; glue in place. ❖

Small Spearmint Leaf
3 holes x 5 holes
Cut 10

Large Spearmint Leaf
5 holes x 8 holes
Cut 2

Heart
3 holes x 3 holes
Cut 6

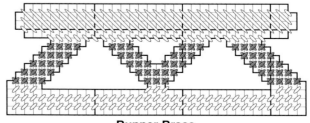

Runner Brace
34 holes x 13 holes
Cut 2, reverse 1 before stitching

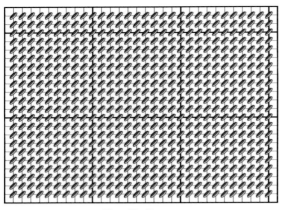

Box Bottom
31 holes x 23 holes
Cut 1

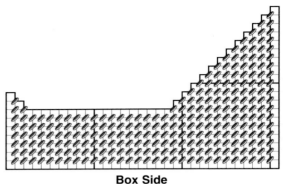

Box Side
31 holes x 19 holes
Cut 2, reverse 1 before stitching

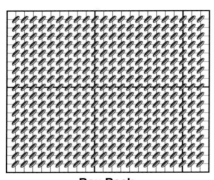

Box Back
23 holes x 19 holes
Cut 1

COLOR KEY	
Plastic Canvas Yarn	**Yards**
☐ White #01	17
◼ Wine #11	10
◼ Brisk green #27	8
◼ Walnut #47	85
#3 Pearl Cotton	
╱ White Backstitch	3
● Very dark Christmas red #498 French Knot	3
● Christmas green #909 French Knot	3

Color numbers given are for Spinrite plastic canvas yarn and DMC #3 pearl cotton.

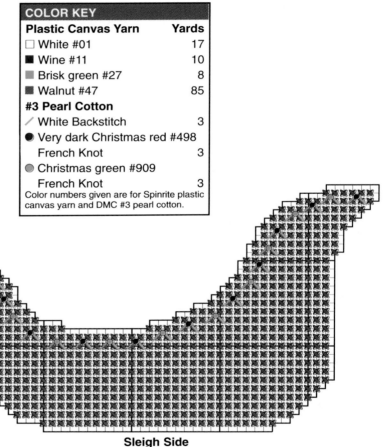

Sleigh Side
58 holes x 29 holes
Cut 2, reverse 1 before stitching

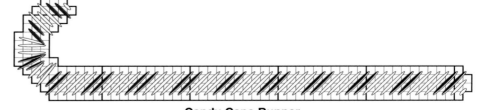

Box Front
23 holes x 9 holes
Cut 1

Candy Cane Runner
52 holes x 12 holes
Cut 2, reverse 1 before stitching

Snowman Candy Caddy
Continued from Page 135

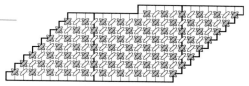

Snowman Arm
27 holes x 9 holes
Cut 2 from 7-count
Reverse 1 before stitching

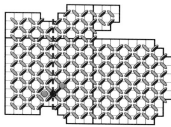

Snowman Mitten
19 holes x 14 holes
Cut 2 from 7-count
Reverse 1 before stitching

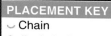

Nose
8 holes x 3 holes
Cut 2 from 10-count
Reverse 1 before stitching

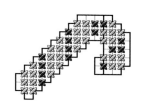

Candy Cane
13 holes x 10 holes
Cut 1 from 10-count

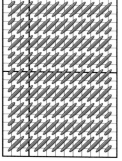

Box Short Side
13 holes x 19 holes ;
Cut 2 from 7-count

Snowman
44 holes x 78 holes
Cut 1 from 7-count

PLACEMENT KEY
- ⌣ Chain
- ◯ Jingle bell
- ● Crystal snowflake
- ◉ Holly leaf
- ⟋ Candy cane
- ∧ Nose
- ▶◀ Bow tie
- ⟋ Green ribbon
- ● Pompon
- ● Round cabochon
- O Oval cabochon

COLOR KEY

4-Ply Yarn	Yards
■ Cranberry	20
■ Christmas red	15
☐ White	15
■ Black	12
■ Bright green	45
Backstitch	
⟋ White	
4mm Braid	
▦ Iridescent	22
#3 Pearl Cotton	
■ White	2
▦ Christmas red #321	4
▦ Light copper #922	1
Backstitch	
⟋ Dark pewter gray #413	1

Color numbers given are for #3 pearl cotton by DMC.

SNOWMAN CANDY CADDY

Designed by Celia Lange Designs

This cheerful snowman is the perfect table decoration for the holidays! Fill the opening with candies, cards or other items of good cheer.

Skill Level: Advanced

Materials

- 2 sheets 7-count plastic canvas
- Scrap pieces 10-count plastic canvas
- 4-ply yarn as listed in color key
- #3 pearl cotton as listed in color key
- 4mm iridescent braid
- 4 (6mm) gold jingle bells
- 2 crystal snowflake gems
- 7 (9mm) round black cabochons
- 2 (14mm x 10mm) oval black cabochons
- 6 (19mm x 10.5mm) emerald holly leaves
- Scraps of gold link chain
- 2 (½") white pompons
- Red-and-white polka-dot bow
- Scrap of ⅜"-wide green satin ribbon
- Lightweight cardboard
- Low-temp glue gun
- Oval glue sticks

Instructions

1. Cut plastic canvas according to graphs (also see Page 133).

2. Stitch all pieces following graphs, reversing one arm, one mitten and one nose piece before stitching. Add backstitching to mittens and hat after background is completed.

3. Whipstitch long straight edges of nose pieces together with light copper #3 pearl cotton. Overcast all other nose edges with light copper.

4. Using green yarn, Overcast top edges of box. Whipstitch box together with green.

5. Using 4-ply yarn, Overcast white areas and arms of snowman with white, and red areas and mittens with cranberry. Overcast hat with black. Overcast candy cane with white #3 pearl cotton.

6. Using snowman as a template, trace and cut cardboard backing. Glue backing to back of snowman.

7. Following placement guide, glue nose, candy cane and all other accessories to snowman and mittens.

8. Using photo as a guide, glue box to body then glue arms and mittens to box. Glue back edges of arms to side edges of snowman, with wrong sides against box. ❖

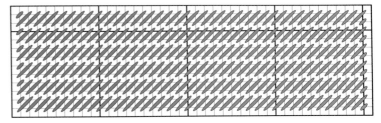

Box Bottom
41 holes x 13 holes
Cut 1 from 7-count

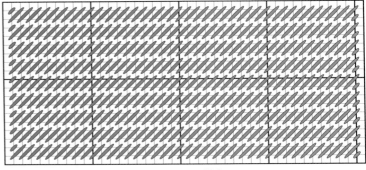

Box Long Side
41 holes x 19 holes
Cut 2 from 7-count

CELESTA

Designed by Dianne Davis

Make this elegant angel the pinnacle of your Christmas tree this year. Her flowing gown and golden wings add to her celestial beauty.

Skill Level: Advanced

Materials

- 2 sheets 10-count plastic canvas
- #3 pearl cotton as listed in color key
- 6-strand embroidery floss as listed in color key
- Heavy (#32) metallic braid as listed in color key
- #22 tapestry needle
- Beading needle
- 113 gold glass seed beads
- 3¼" porcelain doll head
- Fishing line or clear plastic thread
- 3" rubber band
- Craft glue

Cutting & Stitching

1. Cut plastic canvas according to graphs (see also Pages 138 and 139).

2. Stitch pieces following graphs. Attach beads with 1 strand Christmas red floss. Overcast all wing edges with gold. Straight Stitch gold braid across wing openings, making sure braid is not twisted.

3. Overcast cape and front sleeve edges and bottom edge of dress between red dots with gold.

4. Align Arm Front A and Arm Back A where indicated on graph with blue dot, then Whipstitch pieces together with Christmas red.

5. Overcast stitched shoulder and remaining sleeve edges with Christmas red and top and bottom edges of hand with light sportsman flesh. Do not overcast unstitched tab or long straight edge of hand. Repeat for remaining arm.

Assembly

1. Insert unstitched arm tabs into corresponding slots on cape. Tack to wrong side of cape with clear plastic thread. *Note: When using clear plastic thread, double the thread and knot end.* Tack upper rear corners of arm backs to cape where indicated on graph with a green dot.

2. Use clear thread to attach Wings E and F to corresponding lines on cape.

3. With wrong side of cape next to right side of dress, align C on cape with C on dress; tack with clear plastic thread. Tack edge of cape along stitched edge of dress, making sure all unstitched areas on that side are covered.

4. Wrap unstitched dress tabs tightly around neck of doll head; secure with clear plastic thread.

5. Bring cape around to front and tack D on cape to D on dress. Tack C and D on cape to each other. Tack edge of cape to dress as in step 3.

6. Whipstitch unstitched edges of hands together with light sportsman flesh. Pinch hands together to form praying hands. With clear plastic thread, tack bottom of hands together to hold in position.

7. Cut a 6" piece of gold braid and tie into a bow. Glue bow at neckline. Trim ends as desired. ❖

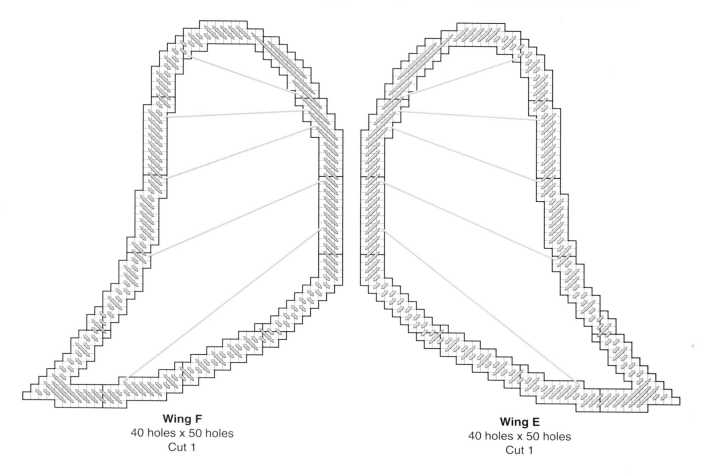

Wing F
40 holes x 50 holes
Cut 1

Wing E
40 holes x 50 holes
Cut 1

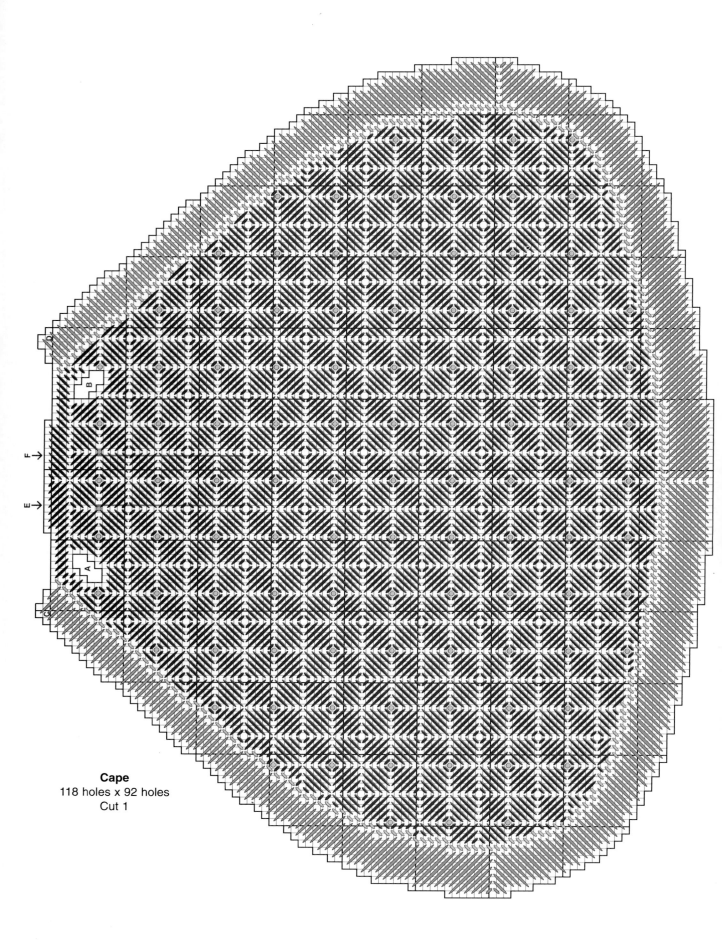

Cape
118 holes x 92 holes
Cut 1

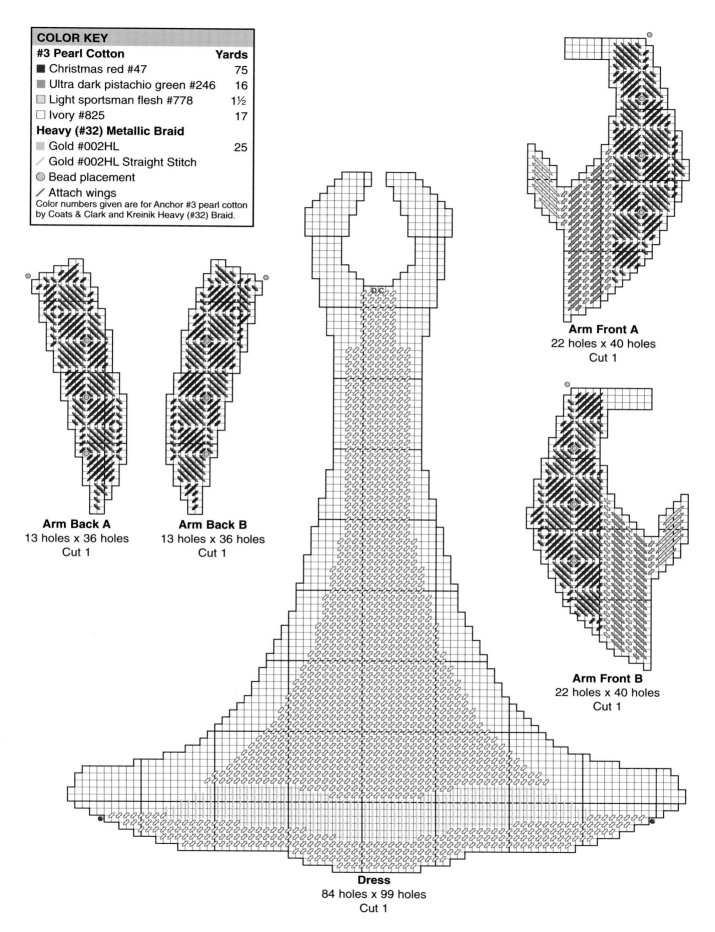

COLOR KEY

#3 Pearl Cotton — Yards

- ■ Christmas red #47 — 75
- ▨ Ultra dark pistachio green #246 — 16
- ▨ Light sportsman flesh #778 — 1½
- □ Ivory #825 — 17

Heavy (#32) Metallic Braid

- ▨ Gold #002HL — 25
- ╱ Gold #002HL Straight Stitch
- ⬤ Bead placement
- ╱ Attach wings

Color numbers given are for Anchor #3 pearl cotton by Coats & Clark and Kreinik Heavy (#32) Braid.

Arm Front A
22 holes x 40 holes
Cut 1

Arm Back A
13 holes x 36 holes
Cut 1

Arm Back B
13 holes x 36 holes
Cut 1

Arm Front B
22 holes x 40 holes
Cut 1

Dress
84 holes x 99 holes
Cut 1

Santa's Little Helpers

Designed by Joan Green

Skill Level: Beginner

Materials

- ¼ sheet 7-count plastic canvas
- Plastic canvas yarn as listed in color key
- 1 yard metallic gold plastic canvas yarn
- 2 (½") white pompons
- #16 tapestry needle
- Hot-glue gun

Instructions

1. Cut plastic canvas according to graphs.

2. Stitch pieces following graphs, Overcasting outer edges with adjacent colors at the same time inner areas are stitched. Overcast tree trunk with walnut. Stitch noses in double Cross Stitches. Use one strand black plastic can-

vas yarn for Backstitching.

3. Glue pompons to ends of caps. Attach yarn to center top if using as ornaments or glue elves to sides of basket. ❖

COLOR KEY

Plastic Canvas Yarn	Yards
☐ Metallic gold	1
☐ White #1	2
☐ Peach #7	3
■ Taupe #20	3
■ Scarlet #22	4
☐ Candy #25	1
■ Brisk green #27	7
■ Black #28	1
■ Walnut #47	1
French Knots	
○ Metallic gold	
● Black	
Backstitch	
╱ Black	

Color numbers given are for Spinrite plastic canvas yarn.

Smiling Elf
22 holes x 31 holes
Cut 1

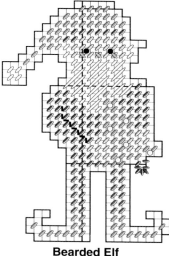

Bearded Elf
21 holes x 31 holes
Cut 1

REINDEE

Designed by Carol Krob

Skill Level: Beginner

Materials

- 3 artist sheets clear 7-count plastic canvas
- Plastic canvas yarn as listed in color key
- ⅛" metallic ribbon as listed in color key
- Pebble beads as listed in color key
- 3 yards ⅜"-wide gold metallic braid
- #18 tapestry needle
- #22 tapestry needle
- Sewing needle and thread

Project Note

When working with metallic ribbon, keep ribbon smooth and flat. To prevent twisting and tangling, guide ribbon between thumb and forefinger of free hand. Drop needle occasionally to let ribbon unwind.

GARLAND

Draped across a fireplace mantel or doorway, Santa's reindeer, including Rudolph, will bring in holiday spirit!

Instructions

1. Cut nine reindeer according to graph (Page 147), rounding off corners.

2. Using #18 tapestry needle for yarn and #22 tapestry needle for ⅛" ribbon, stitch reindeer following graph. Change saddles for each reindeer, following graphs. Attach pebble beads with Half Cross Stitches while working ribbon portion of design.

3. Stitch collars with gold and the dominant color of saddle. With red ribbon, work nine Cross Stitches, three across and three down, for Rudolph's nose. Overcast edges with gold ribbon.

4. To make harness, loop braid around each reindeer's nose; secure loop with a small stitch, using sewing needle and thread. Braid should skim lower edge of saddles when reindeer are placed about 1" apart. ❖

Nutcracker Ballet Ornaments

Designed by Alida Macor

The Nutcracker, Maria and the Sugarplum Fairy make a treasured trio of ornaments. Beautiful design with detailed stitching make all three lifelike.

Skill Level: Intermediate

Materials

- 1 sheet 10-count plastic canvas
- #3 pearl cotton as listed in color key
- 6-strand embroidery floss as listed in color key
- Metallic ribbon floss as listed in color key
- 13 (3mm) gold beads
- ½ yard ⅜"-wide white gathered lace
- ¼ yard medium blue tulle
- ½ yard ¼"-wide medium blue ribbon
- Transparent sewing thread
- Monofilament line
- Yellow or gold plastic sword-shaped toothpick
- Straight pins

Maria

1. Cut plastic canvas according to graphs.

2. Stitch pieces following graphs, leaving tail of black yarn on back piece for Whipstitching to front piece. With transparent sewing thread, attach gold beads where indicated on graph.

3. With wrong sides together, Whipstitch shoe edges together with black. Whipstitch remaining edges together with adjacent colors, except for bottom of skirt between legs.

4. With transparent thread, sew gathered lace around wrists for cuffs and around top of bottom skirt tier (see photo).

5. Thread monofilament through top center hole; tie ends in a knot to form a loop for hanging.

The Nutcracker

1. Cut plastic canvas according to graphs.

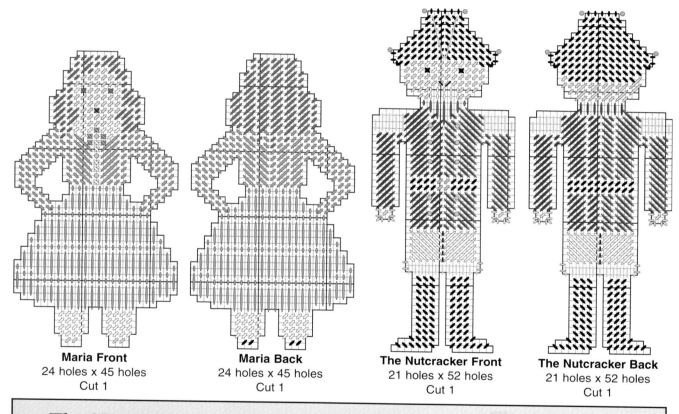

Maria Front
24 holes x 45 holes
Cut 1

Maria Back
24 holes x 45 holes
Cut 1

The Nutcracker Front
21 holes x 52 holes
Cut 1

The Nutcracker Back
21 holes x 52 holes
Cut 1

The Nutcracker Ballet

Adapted from *The Tales of Hoffman* (1816), *The Nutcracker Ballet* is a perennial favorite at Christmas. This enchanting story revolves around a little girl's dream on Christmas Eve:

There was always a party at 7-year-old Maria's house the night before Christmas, and godfather Drosselmeyer always brought the most intriguing presents.

This year he brings Maria a wooden nutcracker that looks like a soldier and can crack nuts between his teeth. Maria loves it!

In a dream that night, Maria returns to the parlor to see Nutcracker. Suddenly mice (common in homes of the era) appear and grow as large as people. Nutcracker and the other toys also grow in size and a battle ensues. Maria repels the mice and saves Nutcracker by throwing her slipper at the King of Mice.

In appreciation, the Nutcracker turns into a prince and escorts Maria to the Land of Sweets. There the reigning Sugarplum Fairy showers her guests with every sweet and treat a little girl could imagine in a dream!

—Alida Macor

2. Stitch pieces following graphs, Overcasting areas shown on graphs only. Backstitch with 2 strands black embroidery floss where indicated on graph. Add gold Straight Stitches on hat front.

3. With transparent sewing thread, attach gold beads where indicated on graph.

4. With wrong sides of Nutcracker together, Whipstitch hat sides together between blue dots with gold and neck area with red. Whipstitch remaining edges together with adjacent colors where not previously Overcast.

5. Cut toothpick so blade is 1⅝" long. Dip strand of black pearl cotton in white craft glue and wrap around pick to simulate a sheath. Attach to belt with transparent thread.

6. Thread monofilament through top center hole; tie ends in a knot to form a loop for hanging.

Sugarplum Fairy

1. Cut pieces according to graphs.

2. Stitch pieces following graphs. Stitch vertical rows of Lattice Stitch on skirt, beginning and ending all yarn under top of gown or under blue trim at bottom. Backstitch with 2 strands black embroidery floss where indicated on graph. Add silver Straight Stitch for band on head.

3. Overcast bottom edges of skirt with white and top edge of each gown strap in silver. With wrong sides together, Whipstitch remaining edges together with adjacent colors.

4. Cut a 6" x 10" piece from tulle. Fold in half lengthwise. Stitch a gathering stitch through both layers of tulle along folded edge. Gather tulle around waist and secure with a few stitches in the back. Cover gathers at waist with blue ribbon. Tie bow in back, trimming ends as desired.

5. Thread monofilament through top center hole; tie ends in a knot to form a loop for hanging. ❖

COLOR KEY	
#3 Pearl Cotton	**Yards**
☐ White	2
■ Black #310	1
■ Medium steel gray #414	1
■ Russet #434	1
☐ Light lemon #445	1
■ Bright Christmas red #666	1
▨ Very light pearl gray #762	1
▨ Medium blue #813	1
■ Medium carnation #892	1
▨ Nile #913	1
☐ Very light peach flesh #948	1
Metallic Ribbon Floss	
▨ Gold #144F-1	
■ Silver #144F-2	
⁄ Gold #144F-1 Straight Stitch	
⁄ Silver #144F-2 Straight Stitch	
6-Strand Embroidery Floss	
⁄ Black #310 Backstitch	
● Attach gold beads	

Color numbers given are for DMC #3 pearl cotton and embroidery floss and Rhode Island Textile metallic RibbonFloss.

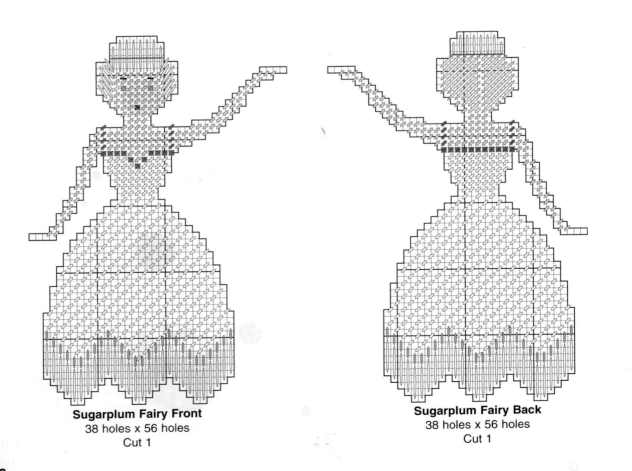

Sugarplum Fairy Front
38 holes x 56 holes
Cut 1

Sugarplum Fairy Back
38 holes x 56 holes
Cut 1

Reindeer Garland
Continued from Page 143

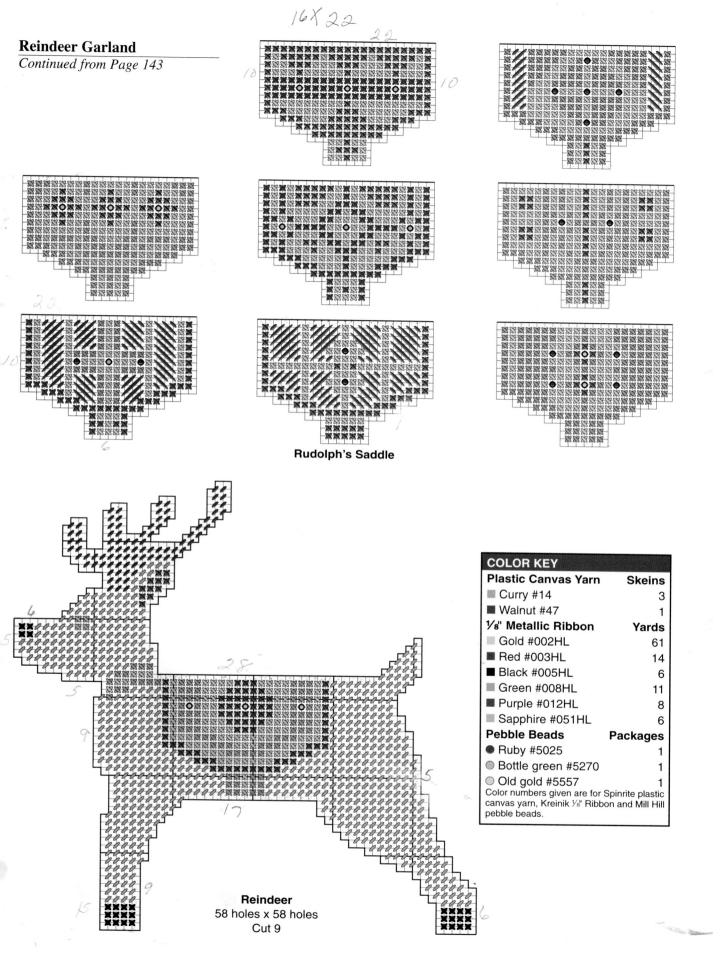

Rudolph's Saddle

Reindeer
58 holes x 58 holes
Cut 9

COLOR KEY

Plastic Canvas Yarn	Skeins
Curry #14	3
Walnut #47	1

⅛" Metallic Ribbon	Yards
Gold #002HL	61
Red #003HL	14
Black #005HL	6
Green #008HL	11
Purple #012HL	8
Sapphire #051HL	6

Pebble Beads	Packages
Ruby #5025	1
Bottle green #5270	1
Old gold #5557	1

Color numbers given are for Spinrite plastic canvas yarn, Kreinik ⅛" Ribbon and Mill Hill pebble beads.

GINGERBREAD HOUSE

Designed by Karen McDanel

Gift-laden sleighs pulled by reindeer circle Santa's charming gingerbread house before flying off to deliver their presents to children around the world!

Skill Level: Advanced

Materials

- 3 sheets regular 7-count plastic canvas
- 1 sheet stiff 7-count plastic canvas
- 4-ply worsted weight yarn as listed in color key
- Metallic cord as listed in color key
- 12" straw wreath
- 8⅓ yards 3-ply 3"-wide pine garland
- 18 (20mm) red wooden beads
- 8 (4mm) movable eyes
- 2 (10mm) round gold beads
- ⅔ yard ¼"-wide red satin ribbon
- Small amount polyester fiberfill
- Hot-glue gun

Cutting & Stitching

1. Cut house front, back and sides from stiff plastic canvas according to graphs (Pages 150 and 151). Cut remaining pieces from regular plastic canvas.

2. Cut one 29-hole x 25-hole piece for house bottom and two 13-hole x 7-hole pieces for sleigh bottoms. House and sleigh bottoms will remain unstitched.

3. Place two base pieces together and stitch through both pieces following graph. Overcast edges with paddy green.

4. Stitch remaining pieces following graphs, reversing two sleigh sides and four reindeer before stitching. Work Backstitches and French Knots over completed stitching.

5. Stitch six of the eight gift box large sides with red cord; two will remain unstitched. Stitch six of the eight gift box medium sides with sliver cord; two will remain unstitched. Stitch 10 of the 20 gift box small sides with gold cord, four with red cord and four with silver cord; two will remain unstitched.

House Assembly

1. Overcast top edges of house front, back and sides with warm brown. Whipstitch front, back and sides together with emerald green in green area and warm brown in brown area. Whipstitch house bottom to house with emerald green.

2. With white, Whipstitch top edges of roof pieces together, then Whipstitch eaves to front and back of roof. Overcast remaining edges with paddy green.

3. With jockey red, Whipstitch chimney front, back and sides together. Overcast top edges with white and bottom edges with jockey red.

4. Cut red satin ribbon into two 12" lengths. Tie each in a bow and glue to center top of wreaths on front and back of house (see photo). Trim ends as desired.

5. Glue gold beads to doors where indicated on graph, and chimney to center of roof; glue fiberfill in chimney to resemble smoke. Roof may be glued in place to top of house or left unattached so house can be used for storing candy.

Small Piece Assembly

1. With jockey red, Whipstitch one sleigh front, back and sides together then Whipstitch sleigh bottom to sleigh. Overcast top edges with jockey red and runners with silver. Repeat for remaining sleigh.

2. For gift boxes, place all sides with matching colors together in a group to form three groups. For each red gift box, Whipstitch three large and two small stitched sides together with red cord, then

Whipstitch one large unstitched side to box for box bottom.

3. For each silver gift box, Whipstitch three medium and two small stitched sides together with silver cord, then Whipstitch one medium unstitched side to box for box bottom.

4. For each gold gift box, Whipstitch five small stitched sides together with gold cord, then Whipstitch one small unstitched side to box for box bottom.

5. Cut two 12" lengths of cord from each of the three colors. Tie gold cord around silver boxes, red cord around gold boxes and silver cord around red boxes (see photo). Glue knots of bows to hold in place.

6. Overcast bottoms of reindeer between blue dots with mid brown. With wrong sides together, Whipstitch one left side to one right side using tan for antlers and chest area and mid brown for remaining unstitched edges. Repeat for remaining reindeer.

7. Glue eyes on reindeer where indicated on graphs.

Centerpiece Assembly

1. Glue pine garland around straw wreath, twisting garland while gluing to give wreath more body. Center and glue finished wreath to base.

2. Glue house to center of base in circle of wreath.

3. Using photo as a guide, glue one silver gift and one gold gift in each sleigh. Glue two reindeer and one sleigh to wreath in front and in back of house. Glue one red gift to wreath at each side of house.

4. Using photo as a guide, glue three wooden beads to side of wreath between each reindeer and sleigh, each sleigh and gift and each gift and reindeer. ❖

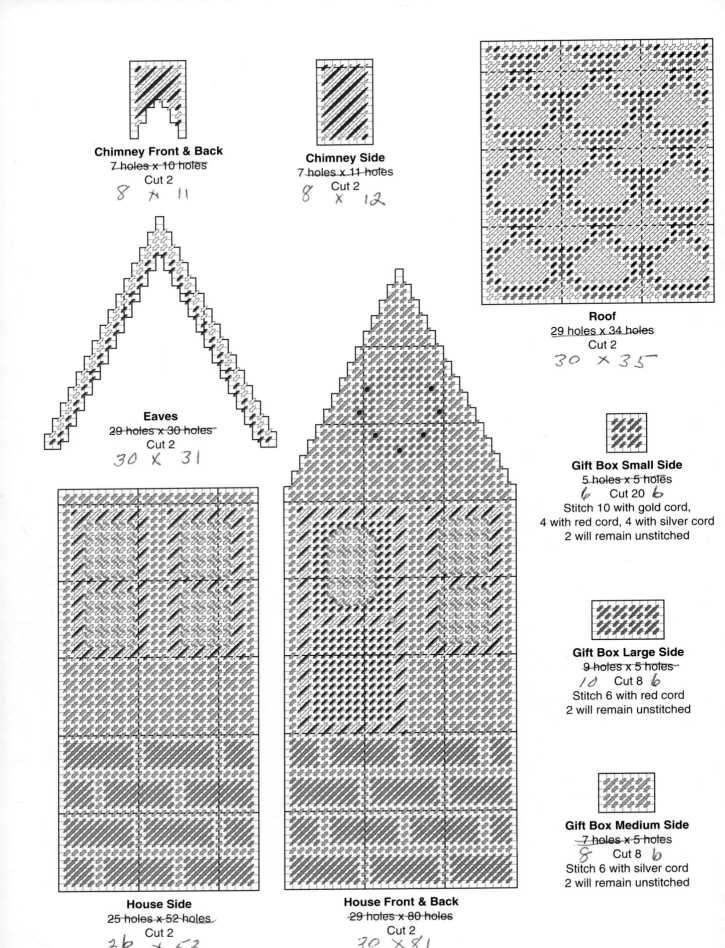

Chimney Front & Back
7 holes x 10 holes
Cut 2
8 x 11

Chimney Side
7 holes x 11 holes
Cut 2
8 x 12

Roof
29 holes x 34 holes
Cut 2
30 x 35

Eaves
29 holes x 30 holes
Cut 2
30 x 31

Gift Box Small Side
5 holes x 5 holes
6 Cut 20 6
Stitch 10 with gold cord,
4 with red cord, 4 with silver cord
2 will remain unstitched

Gift Box Large Side
9 holes x 5 holes
10 Cut 8 6
Stitch 6 with red cord
2 will remain unstitched

Gift Box Medium Side
7 holes x 5 holes
8 Cut 8 6
Stitch 6 with silver cord
2 will remain unstitched

House Side
25 holes x 52 holes
Cut 2
26 x 53

House Front & Back
29 holes x 80 holes
Cut 2
30 x 81

150

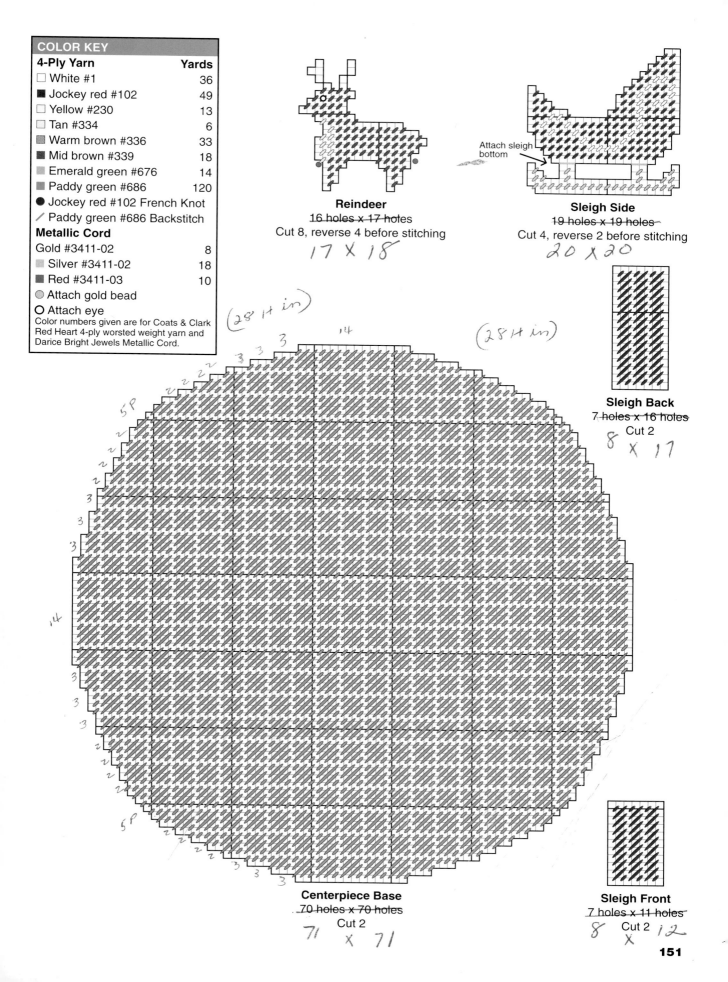

Reindeer
16 holes x 17 holes
Cut 8, reverse 4 before stitching
17 X 18

Sleigh Side
19 holes x 19 holes
Cut 4, reverse 2 before stitching
20 X 20

Attach sleigh bottom

Sleigh Back
7 holes x 16 holes
Cut 2
8 X 17

(28 ½ in)   *14*   *(28 ½ in)*

14

Centerpiece Base
70 holes x 70 holes
Cut 2
71 X 71

Sleigh Front
7 holes x 11 holes
Cut 2
8 X 12

151

SANTA GIFT BAG

Designed by Michele Wilcox

Tuck a small gift into this cute gift bag!
With his twinkling blue eyes and jinglebell stocking,
this Santa is sure to make someone's day!

Skill Level: Beginner

Materials

- 1¼ sheets 7-count plastic canvas
- Plastic canvas yarn as listed in color key
- 12" ¼"-wide off-white double-faced satin ribbon
- ⅝" jingle bell
- Hot-glue gun

Instructions

1. Cut plastic canvas according to graphs.

2. On mustache, Overcast mouth area with cinnamon where indicated on graph and remaining edges with white. With holly green Overcast handle edges and top edges of bag sides. Overcast nose and Santa's face with adjacent colors.

3. With holly green, Whipstitch bag sides together and then bottom to sides; tack handle to top center of bag large sides or glue in place.

4. Using photo as a guide, center and glue mustache below flesh tone area on face, then glue nose to face and mustache.

5. Sew jingle bell to Santa where indicated on graph, then tie bow around attaching yarn with off-white ribbon. Glue Santa's face to one large side. ❖

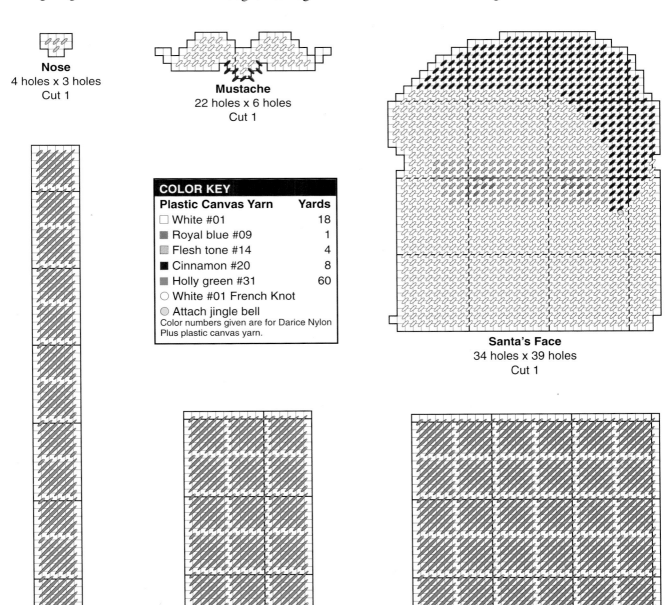

Nose
4 holes x 3 holes
Cut 1

Mustache
22 holes x 6 holes
Cut 1

Santa's Face
34 holes x 39 holes
Cut 1

COLOR KEY	
Plastic Canvas Yarn	**Yards**
☐ White #01	18
◼ Royal blue #09	1
▨ Flesh tone #14	4
◼ Cinnamon #20	8
◼ Holly green #31	60
◯ White #01 French Knot	
◯ Attach jingle bell	
Color numbers given are for Darice Nylon Plus plastic canvas yarn.	

Bag Handle
6 holes x 66 holes
Cut 1

Bag Bottom & Small Side
16 holes x 31 holes
Cut 3

Bag Large Side
31 holes x 31 holes
Cut 2

Stitch Key

Use the following diagrams to expand your plastic canvas stitching. For each diagram, bring needle up through canvas at the red number one and go back down through the canvas at the red number two. The second stitch is numbered in green. Always bring needle up through the canvas at odd numbers and take it back down through the canvas at the even numbers.

Background Stitches

The following stitches are used for filling in large areas of canvas. The Continental Stitch is the most commonly used stitch. Other stitches, such as the Condensed Mosaic and Scotch Stitch, fill in large areas of canvas more quickly than the Continental Stitch because their stitches cover a larger area of canvas.

Alternating Continental

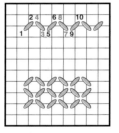

Condensed Mosaic

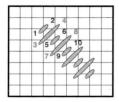

Continental Stitch

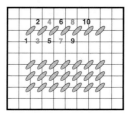

Cross Stitch

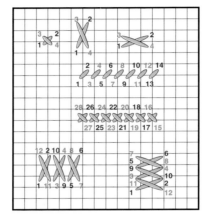

Long Stitch

Scotch Stitch

Slanting Gobelin

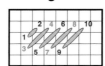

Embroidery Stitches

Embroidery stitches are worked on top of a stitched area to add detail and beauty to your project. Embroidery stitches are usually worked with one strand of yarn, several strands of pearl cotton or several strands of embroidery floss.

Back Stitch

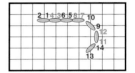

Chain Stitch

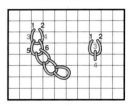

Couching

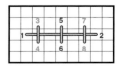

Fly Stitch

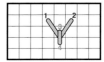

Lattice Stitch

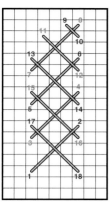

Lazy Daisy

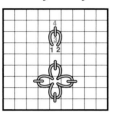

Straight Stitch

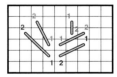

Specialty Stitches

The following stitches can be worked either on top of a previously stitched area or directly onto the canvas. Like the embroidery stitches, these too add wonderful detail and give your stitching additional interest and texture.

Diamond Eyelet

For each stitch, bring needle up at odd numbers around outside and take needle down through canvas at center hole.

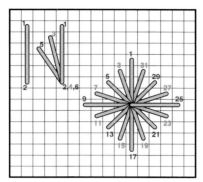

Loop Stitch (Turkey Loop Stitch)

The top diagram shows this stitch left in tact. This is an effective stitch for giving a project dimensional hair. The bottom diagram demonstrates the cut loop stitch. Because each stitch is anchored, cutting it will not cause the stitches to come out. A group of cut loop stitches give a fluffy, soft look and feel to your project.

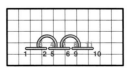

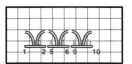

Satin Stitch

This stitch gives a "padded" look to your work.

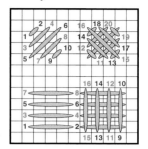

Smyrna Cross

Parisian Stitch

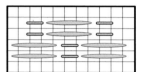

Finishing Stitches

Both of these stitches are used to finish the outer edges of the canvas. Overcasting is done to finish one edge at a time. Whipstitch is used to stitch two pieces of canvas together. For both Overcasting and Whipstitching, work one stitch in each hole along straight edges and inside corners, and two or three stitches in outside corners.

Overcast/ Whipstitch

Index

Special Thanks

As with the production of any book, the success of the publication depends on the quality of the content. The publishers and editorial staff of *Festival of Holiday Plastic Canvas* would like to give recognition to each of the designers whose marvelous designs have filled the pages of this plastic canvas craft book. We appreciate their efforts and admire their talent.

**Celia Lange &
Martha Bleidner
of Celia Lange Designs**

Autumn Harvest
Christmas Jewelry
Elegant Embroidered Eggs
Hanukkah Dreidel
Ice Castle Ornament
Jack-o'-Lantern Coasters
Peppermint Sleigh
Pot-o'-Gold Candy Dish
Snowman Candy Caddy

Vicki Blizzard

Add a Little Sparkle
Christmas Critters
Easter Egg Surprises

Mary Cosgrove

Day-by-Day Calendar
Lucky the Leprechaun
Potpourri Pumpkin
World's Best Dad

Dianne Davis

Celesta
Curly the Clown
Easter Egg Hunt
Songbird

Darla Fanton

Harvest Welcome
Proud to be Irish

Joan Green

Sparkling Shamrocks
Plaid Desk Organizer
Santa's Little Helpers

Carol Krob

Reindeer Garland

Alida Macor

Nutcracker Ballet Ornaments

Nancy Marshall

Bunny & Chick Basket Buddies
Eggs in a Basket
Love Notes
Summer Picnic

Karen McDanel

All-American Mug
Gingerbread House
World's Best Mom
Classic Car

Adele Mogavero

Jelly Bean Buddies

Ruth Schmuff

Confetti Coasters

Trudy Bath Smith

Carrot Patch Candy Dish
Leprechaun Party

Rosemarie Walter

Glow Totes

Michele Wilcox

Candy Hearts for Sweethearts
Cornucopia Place Mat
Little Pilgrim
Santa Gift Bag
Teddy Bear's Thanksgiving
Thanksgiving Place
Card Holders
Uncle Sam's Bank
Valentine Cupids

Lois Winston

Gift Box Planter

Kathy Wirth

Bat Candy Keeper
Forever Yours Keepsake Box
Golden Diamonds Gift Box
Stars & Stripes Jewelry

Linda Wyszynski

Shimmery Blue Earrings

Acknowledgments

Our gratitude is extended to all who opened up their homes and businesses for the photography of this book. The beautiful locations added delightful warmth, charm and personality to the photographs.

- Limberlost Society, Geneva, Indiana
- Schug House Inn, Berne, Indiana

We'd also like to thank the following manufacturers who have generously provided our designers with materials and supplies. We appreciate their contribution to the production of this book.

AdTech
- Crafty Magic Melt glue—Pot o' Gold Candy Dish, Jack-o'-Lantern Coasters, Autumn Harvest
- Crafty Magic Melt glue gun—Jelly Bean Bunnies, Snowman Candy Caddy
- Duchess glue gun—Peppermint Sleigh
- Princess glue gun—Pot o' Gold Candy Dish, Jack-o'-Lantern Coasters, Autumn Harvest, Hanukkah Dreidel, Ice Castle Ornament

The Beadery
- Acrylic gems—Ice Castle Ornament
- Cabochons—Easter Egg Surprise, Jelly Bean Bunnies, Christmas Critters, Snowman Candy Caddy
- Holly leaves—Snowman Candy Caddy

Bedford Industries
- Bendable Ribbon—Black Cat Wreath

The Caron Collection
- Watercolor Yarn—Shimmery Blue Earrings

Clearly Lucite
- 173 Boutique Tissue—World's Greatest Dad

Coats & Clark
- Anchor® #3 pearl cotton—Celesta
- Anchor® 6-strand embroidery floss—Bat Candy Keeper, Celesta
- Red Heart Classic yarn—Classic Car Keeper, All-American Mug, Gingerbread House

Creative Crystals Co.
- BeJeweler™ rhinestone setter— Easter Egg Surprise
- Crystal rhinestones—Easter Egg Surprise

Daniel Enterprises
- Crafter's Pride Stitch-A-Mug™—Proud to be Irish, World's Best Mom, All-American Mug

Darice
- Beads—Leprechaun Party
- Bright Jewels Metallic Cord—Leprechaun Party, Classic Car Keeper, Gingerbread House
- Crystal snowflake gems—Snowman Candy Caddy
- Jingle bells—Snowman Candy Caddy
- Nylon Plus™ plastic canvas yarn—Pot o' Gold Candy Dish, Love Notes, Leprechaun Party, Bunny & Chick Basket Buddies, Eggs in a Basket, Carrot Patch Candy Dish, Santa Gift Bag
- Plastic canvas—Proud to be Irish, Love Notes, Leprechaun Party, Easter Egg Surprise, Elegant Embroidered Eggs, Easter Egg Hunt, Eggs in a Basket, Jelly Bean Bunnies, Carrot Patch Candy Dish, Songbird, Classic Car Keeper, Shimmery Blue Earrings, Summer Picnic, Jack-o'-Lantern Coasters, Curly the Clown, Bat Candy Keeper, Teddy Bear's Thanksgiving, Christmas Critters, Hanukkah Dreidel, Snowman Candy Caddy, Celesta, Gingerbread House
- Plastic canvas Crafty Circle—Bat Candy Keeper
- Plastic canvas circle—Carrot Patch Candy Dish
- Straw Satin Raffia—Eggs in a Basket, Harvest Welcome
- Ultra Stiff plastic canvas—Plaid Desk Organizer, Summer Picnic, Black Cat Wreath, Autumn Harvest, Harvest Welcome, Gingerbread House

DecoArt
- Americana acrylic paint—Hanukkah Dreidel

Delta
- Jewel Glue—Lucky the Leprechaun

DMC
- #3 pearl cotton—Proud to be Irish, Countdown Coasters, Elegant Embroidered Eggs, Jack-o'-Lantern Coasters, Autumn Harvest, Teddy Bear's Thanksgiving, Peppermint Sleigh, Snowman Candy Caddy, Nutcracker Ballet Ornaments
- #5 pearl cotton—Elegant Embroidered Eggs, Jack-o'-Lantern Coasters, Autumn Harvest
- 6-strand embroidery floss—Easter Egg Hunt, Bunny & Chick Basket Buddies, Shimmery Blue Earrings, Autumn Harvest, Christmas Jewelry, Nutcracker Ballet Ornaments

Eclectic Products Inc.
- Craftsman's Goop®—

Songbird, Curly the Clown, Celesta

Fibre-Craft
- Porcelain doll head—Celesta

Kreinik
- ⅛" Ribbon—Confetti Coasters, Forever Yours Keepsake Box, Glow Totes, Reindeer Garland
- Fine (#8) Braid—Bat Candy Keeper, Christmas Critters
- Heavy (#32) Braid—Lucky the Leprechaun, Celesta
- Medium (#16) Braid—Shimmery Blue Earrings, Glow Totes

Kunin Felt Co./Foss Mfg.
- Felt—Leprechaun Party
- Presto felt—Forever Yours Keepsake Box, Songbird, Golden Diamonds Gift Box, Bat Candy Keeper

Madeira
- Braid—Pot o' Gold Candy Dish
- Braid Plus Two—Ice Castle Ornament
- Braid Ribbon 2—Pot o' Gold Candy Dish
- Braid Ribbon 4—Pot o' Gold Candy Dish
- Glimmer metallic thread—Pot o' Gold Candy Dish
- GlissenGloss Braid—Christmas Jewelry, Snowman Candy Caddy
- GlissenGloss Braid Plus Four—Golden Diamonds Gift Box, Stars & Stripes Jewelry

Mangelsen's
- 3" bird—Songbird

MPR
- Satin Raffia Ribbon™—Summer Picnic

Mill Hill/Gay Bowles
- Bugle beads—Elegant Embroidered Eggs
- Frosted glass beads—Elegant Embroidered Eggs

- Pebble beads—Reindeer Garland
- Seed Beads—Shimmery Blue Earrings, Celesta

The New Berlin Co.
- Country Jar Keepers—Lucky the Leprechaun

Rainbow Gallery
- Metallic plastic canvas yarn—Santa's Little Helpers
- Metallic #7 plastic canvas yarn—Sparkling Shamrocks, Plaid Desk Organizer, Santa's Little Helpers

Rhode Island Textile
- RibbonFloss™—Lucky the Leprechaun, Nutcracker Ballet Ornaments

Spinrite
- Bernat® Berella "4"® worsted weight yarn—Harvest Welcome
- Bernat plastic canvas yarn—Golden Diamonds Gift Box, Reindeer Garland
- Spinrite plastic canvas yarn—Forever Yours Keepsake Box, Sparkling Shamrocks, Easter Egg Surprise, Songbird, Plaid Desk Organizer, Autumn Harvest, Christmas Critters, Hanukkah Dreidel, Peppermint Sleigh, Santa's Little Helpers

St. Louis Trimming
- Metallic braid—Reindeer Garland

Uniek
- Needloft® plastic canvas yarn—Day-by-Day Calendar, Lucky the Leprechaun, Candy Hearts for Sweethearts, Valentine Cupids, Easter Egg Hunt, World's Greatest Dad, Patriotic Uncle Sam, Uncle Sam's Bank, Potpourri Pumpkin, Curly the Clown, Black Cat Wreath, Cornucopia Place Mat, Little Pilgrim, Thanksgiving Place Card Holders, Teddy Bear's

Thanksgiving
- Needloft® plastic canvas cord—Lucky the Leprechaun, Carrot Patch Candy Dish, World's Greatest Dad, Patriotic Uncle Sam
- Plastic canvas—Potpourri Pumpkin
- Plastic canvas circle—Leprechaun Party, Potpourri Pumpkin
- Plastic canvas hearts—Forever Yours Keepsake Box
- Plastic Canvas hexagons—Golden Diamonds Gift Box
- Plastic canvas stars—Stars & Stripes Jewelry
- Quick-Count™ plastic canvas—Day-by-Day Calendar, Lucky the Leprechaun, World's Greatest Dad

Westrim Crafts
- Fun Foam—Jack-o'-Lantern Coasters, Peppermint Sleigh
- Jewelry findings—Shimmery Blue Earrings
- Moving eyes—Curly the Clown
- Pompons—Curly the Clown
- Wooden beads—Gingerbread House

Wichelt Imports
- Ceramic button—Gift Box Planter

Wimpole Street Creations
- Fabric yo-yos—Golden Diamonds Gift Box

Wm. E. Wright
- Satin Ribbon—Pot o' Gold Candy Dish, Forever Yours Keepsake Box, Elegant Embroidered Eggs

Notes